HOW HIGH SCHOOL RUNNERS TRAIN

by Frank P. Calore

tafnews

Book Division of Track & Field News

Production Staff: Grace Light, Esther Reeves, Scott Deacon

Jacket Design: Scott Deacon.

Standard Book Number: 0-911521-04-6.

Printed in the United States of America.

PHOTO CREDITS

2

CONTENTS

INTRODUCTION

Once again I ask, "Why is it that some high school athletes develop into outstanding runners? What is it that sets them apart from the plodders, the average runners, and even from the good ones—those who always get the points you need—to become the great ones, the champions, the All-Americans?"

We find that some great runners are great athletes, some are good runners who did the "extra," who put in more work than anyone else and made themselves great, and some are simply blessed with the talent to move faster than all others. In How High School Runners Train, *I have tried to profile all of these types. Great athletes must take that overall talent and sharpen the edges of speed and endurance. Hard workers are a coach's joy and dilemma—they set great examples for an entire team, but their training program must be delicately balanced to prevent injury and mental fatigue. Performance must peak at the proper time. The runner with great natural speed must develop pace knowledge and the competitive skills to be in position to use that speed.*

I sent questionnaires to the nation's outstanding runners and to coaches who, year-in and year-out, produce quality relay teams, and once again I found that high school athletes and their coaches have important things to say about training techniques. Wherever possible I have used their words to describe their preparation and training methods. They have made adjustments for regional weather conditions, for school facilities, and for fluctuating dual-meet and invitational competition schedules. They have developed programs that worked for them. Other athletes and other coaches can use these programs as a framework around which to design their own programs for running success.

Thank you to everyone who contributed material to this project. I hope that your knowledge and skills will help others run to the outstanding levels of achievement that you have reached in your prep careers. Best of luck and continued success to all of you.

Frank P. Calore

ABOUT THE AUTHOR

Frank P. Calore is currently the cross-country and track coach and a social studies teacher at Acton-Boxborough Regional High School in Massachusetts. He is a graduate of the University of Massachusetts with a BA in History and Fitchburg State College with an MEd in Leadership and Management.

Lacking competitive track experience, Frank searched for coaching tips from other coaches, clinics, and books. *How They Train: High School Field Events* (Tafnews Press, 1980) and *How High School Runners Train* represent extensions of this search and the desire to pass the information on to other coaches and athletes.

Frank feels that, while high school athletics help teach valuable lessons, they should also be fun for the athletes and coaches. The high school years are too important to be dominated by total concentration in one area, and everything must be viewed in its proper perspective.

MIDDLE DISTANCE/ DISTANCE

Jim Ailshie

JAMES COLLIER AILSHIE   Dobyns-Bennett High School

Born 8/8/63   Kingsport, Tennessee

6-1   153   Coach Tom Coughenour

COMPETITIVE BACKGROUND

Too small for football, Jim went out for cross-country as a freshman after winning several races in middle school. Jim was State Champion in the mile and 800 meters and was named to All-State Cross-Country and All-State and All-American track teams, and he won the Florida Relays High School 1500 and the Vol Classic High School Mile and 800 Championships. In 1981, Jim was No. 1 on the U.S. 1500 list.

BEST TIMES

49.6(m)   1:50.2(m)   3:49.25(1500m)   4:08.97
8:38.4(3000m)   9:14.2

AGE GROUP MARKS

Year	Age	400	800	1500/Mile	3000/2-Mile
1978	14	58.4	2:08.2	4:38.3	10:00.1
1979	15	53.5	1:59.7	4:26.0	
1980	16	51.8	1:56.46	4:16.4	9:14.2
1981	17	49.6	1:50.2	3:49.25/	8:38.4/9:27.1
				4:08.97	

PREPARATION

Jim warms up for practice by jogging and stretching.

The night before competition he eats pasta and stays away from greasy foods. To warm up for races, he jogs, stretches, and strides 5x110.

During winter and summer Jim works with weights twice each week, concentrating on upper body strength.

Dips 4x10   Curls 5x12   45lb.

Bench Press   5x12   110lb.

Tricep Lift with weight behind head   max reps 15lb.

TRAINING COMMENTS

Jim feels that working with an easy day-hard day training program has allowed him to become a stronger runner. Preferring speed work to distance, he feels the hard-easy pattern allowed him to train extra hard on speedwork days.

DAILY SEASONAL WORKOUTS

Fall

Monday—5-mile run at easy 7:00 pace on hills (AM). 7-mile run at 6:30 pace (PM).

Tuesday—5-mile run (AM). Jog 1 mile; 4x100; 4x200; 4x300 on hills, jog 1 mile between sets; jog 1 mile (PM).

Wednesday—5-mile run (AM). 5-mile run at 6:30 pace (PM).

Thursday—5-mile run (AM). Jog 1 mile; 10x400 (65 seconds) with 1-minute rest between each; 1 mile jog (PM).

Friday—5-mile run (AM).

Saturday—Competition.

Sunday—7-mile run on mountain ridge.

Winter

Monday—7-mile easy run.

Tuesday—7-mile run; weight training.

Wednesday—jog 1 mile; 45 minute "goat trail" run. (Dobyns-Bennett has a 6,000-seat dome with 20 steps each aisle. The workout runs up the aisle, across between the seats, down the next aisle, across the bottom, and back up the steps, continuing the pattern around the dome.)

Thursday—7-mile easy run; weight training.
Friday—Jog 1 mile, 45 minute "goat trail" run; 1-mile jog.
Saturday—5-mile fartlek run.
Sunday—9-mile run at 6:30 pace; weight training.

Spring

Monday—7-mile run at 6:30 pace over hills.
Tuesday—Jog 1-mile, 10x400 under 60 seconds with a 3 minute rest between each; jog 1 mile; weight training.
Wednesday—7-mile easy run.
Thursday—Jog 1 mile; 15x200 in 27-28 seconds with a 200 jog between each and a 4-minute break after 8; jog 1 mile; weight training.
Friday—5-mile jog.
Saturday—Competition—jog in the morning if the race is at night.
Sunday—8-mile easy jog.

Summer

Monday—7-mile run; weight training.
Tuesday—7-mile run.
Wednesday—8-mile run.
Thursday—5-mile run; weight training.
Friday—7-mile run.
Saturday—5-mile run under 6:00 pace.
Sunday—7-mile run.

Jon Butler

JON WILLIAM BUTLER   Edison High School

Born 9/7/62   Huntington Beach, California

6-1   155   Coach Colin McConnell

COMPETITIVE BACKGROUND
Jon began running as a freshman, and became a 1980 cross-country All-American and two time All-Orange County performer. He won the State 3200 in 1981 and led the nation in the 3000 and 2-mile.

BEST TIMES
        1:57(y)   3:52.0(1500m)   4:08.20 (mile)
                8:17.5(3k)   8:49.86(2M)

AGE GROUP MARKS

Year	Age	1500/Mile	3000/2-Mile	3-Mile XC	10K roads
1978	15	4:39(1 mile)	10:14(2 mile)	16:55	
1979	16	4:22(1 mile)	9:06.5(2 mile)	15:09	33:30
1980	17	3:55.4(1500)	8:57.57(2 mile)	14:21	30:41
1981	18	3:52.0/14:08.20	8:17.5/8:49.86	14:52(5k)	29:37

PREPARATION
Jon works out with weights twice each week, doing 2 sets of 20 reps of Bench Press, Tricep Extensions, Uprows, Curls, and Military Press.

To psych up for races, Butler tries to imagine the race, as well as to listen to music, and read about races.

TRAINING COMMENTS
If he could "do it over again," Jon would keep his

distance running and weight program up until late season.

He thinks that hard distance runs with fast runners, long hills, and fartlek running have been the most important part of his training.

DAILY SEASONAL WORKOUTS

Fall

October 6-12, 1980

Monday—4-mile run (AM). 6x330 loop with hill; 10x500 loop continual running alternating 1 hard, 1 easy (PM).

Tuesday—5-mile run (AM). 10.5-mile run (6 miles of run at 32:50) (PM).

Wednesday—5-mile run (AM).

Thursday—5.5-mile run (AM). Dual Meet-3 miles (1st-15:05).
Friday—5-mile run (AM). 7 mile run (PM).
Saturday—4-mile warmup; 3x1 mile on course (4:43, 4:33, 4:27), 4x400 at good pace with 90 second rest between (AM). 4-mile run (PM).
Sunday—10-mile run in hills.

Winter
January 21-27, 1980
Monday—8-mile run.
Tuesday—8-mile run, including 5x430 yard hill.
Wednesday—8-mile run.
Thursday—10-mile run, including 4 fast miles.
Friday—13.5-mile run.
Saturday—10-mile run.
Sunday—12.5-mile run.

Spring
April 14-20, 1980
Monday—6-mile run (AM). 6x440 (61-63 seconds); 6x330 (46-47 seconds); 6x220 (28-29 seconds) (PM).
Tuesday—Easy 9-mile run.
Wednesday—5-mile run (AM). Dual Meet-1 mile (1st 4:31.7) and 2-mile (1st 9:56).
Thursday—Rest.
Friday—Mt. SAC Relays—800 meters (1:57.4) and 1600 meters (4:16.8).
Saturday—Easy 5-mile run.
Sunday—Knotts Berry Farm 10K (9th-31:17).

Summer
July 14-20, 1980
Monday—7-mile run.
Tuesday—11-mile run.
Wednesday—7-mile run, including 3 miles on soft sand.
Thursday—5-mile run.
Friday—2-mile run.
Saturday—AAU Junior Olympics 3000 meters (1st regional—8:37.8).
Sunday—Rest.

Vickie Cook

VICTORIA ELIZABETH COOK   Alemany High School

Born 5/29/64   Mission Hills, California

5-8   98   Coaches Jon Sutherland
                                    Randy Smith

COMPETITIVE BACKGROUND

One of the premier female prep distance runners in the U.S., Vickie began running with her father as an 8-year-old in age group competition. In her career she has been California State Champion at 3200 meters, Pan-Am Junior 3000 Champion, National Junior 3000 runner-up, Western Regional Kinney Cross-Country Champion, and has three undefeated seasons in California cross-country competition.

BEST TIMES

        58.0   2:13   4:41.8(1 mile)   9:22.0(3000m)
        10:14(2 mile)   35:04(10K roads)

AGE GROUP MARKS

Year	Age	880	Mile	3000/2-Mile	10k roads
1975	10	2:23	5:08.9		
1976	11	2:21	5:02.1		
1977	12	2:17	4:55.1		
1978	13	2:16	4:53.0	10:40(2 mile)	
1979	14		4:51.5	10:20(2 mile)	36:10
1980	15		4:49		35:52
1981	16	2:13	4:41.8	9:22/10:14	35:04

PREPARATION

Vickie does regular stretching exercises daily and warms

up with jogging, stretching, and strides before practice and competition. She has no regular weight training program and states her training diet ranges from "junky to healthy."

TRAINING COMMENTS
"Being consistent—ruhning even when I feel terrible, and doing all kinds of runs from distance to sprinting" have been the most important parts of Vickie's training. Before competition, she tries to visualize the race and think about strategy, generally preferring to run a fast, even pace, but occasionally waiting and kicking at the finish.

DAILY SEASONAL WORKOUTS

Fall
Monday—Hard run on the roads.
Tuesday—3x1 mile (under 5:15).
Wednesday—Long 10-mile run with hills.
Thursday—Dual meet, used as an interval workout.
Friday—Rest, easy 4-5 mile run.
Saturday—Invitational Competition or 8-10 mile run.
Sunday—10-14-mile run.
Average 80 miles each week.

Winter
Same basic workouts as in the fall, running in a few indoor meets. Average 80-90 miles each week.

Spring
Monday—Long intervals, 3 x 880(2:28); 4x440(66).
Tuesday—Easy 8-mile run.
Wednesday—Interval ladder, 660-440-330-220, run faster than Monday.
Thursday—Dual meet—speed work after.
Friday—Rest, easy distance, stride 100's.
Saturday—Invitational Competition.
Sunday—10-12 mile run.

Summer
Try to run 70-90 miles each week, running hard two days each week.

Laurie Glynn

LAURA J. GLYNN

Winchester High School

Born 1/11/66

Winchester, Massachusetts

5-5   99

Coaches Joseph Cantillon
Thomas Kline
Lorin Maloney

COMPETITIVE BACKGROUND

Laurie has won numerous honors since she began competing at age 12, including the State Divisional Cross Country and New England High School Mile Championships, New England Junior Olympic Titles and the New England TAC Women's 1000 Championship. Glynn was a national speedskating champion in 1978, and track serves as her dry-land training for skating.

BEST TIMES

2:41(1000)   4:36.8(1500m)   4:54.19   9:46.1(3000m)

AGE GROUP MARKS

Year	Age	1000	1500	Mile	3000
1978	11			5:17	
1979	12			5:04	10:21
1980	13		4:39	4:58	
1981	14	2:41	4:36.8	4:54.19	9:46.1

PREPARATION

Listening to music and concentrating on the race and times prepares Laurie mentally for races. She warms up with a 1-1½ mile jog, 4-6 pick-ups and stretching.

TRAINING COMMENTS

"Consistency" is the most important part of Laurie's training, and she enjoys all of her workout—speedwork, hills, and distance.

DAILY SEASONAL WORKOUTS

Fall
Monday—5-6 miles moderate (7:30 pace).
Tuesday—Cross country race—dual meet.
Wednesday—5-6 miles moderate (7:30 pace).
Thursday—5-6 miles moderate (7:30 pace).
Friday—Cross country race—dual meet.
Saturday—Speedwork-440s and 880s.
Sunday—8 miles easy (7:45 pace).

Winter
Monday—5-6 miles moderate (7:30 pace).
Tuesday—Speedwork-440s, 330s, 660s, 880s early season,
440s, 330s, 220s, late season.
Wednesday—5-6 miles moderate (7:30 pace).
Thursday—2x660; 4½-mile run.
Friday—5 miles easy (7:45 pace).
Saturday—Dual meet.
Sunday—8 miles easy (7:45 pace).

Spring
Monday—5-6 miles moderate (7:30 pace).
Tuesday—Dual meet.
Wednesday—5-6 miles moderate (7:30 pace).
Thursday—Dual meet.
Friday—5-6 miles moderate (7:30 pace).
Saturday—Speedwork-440s, 330s, 220s, or hills.
Sunday—8 miles easy (7:45 pace).

Summer
Monday—6 miles moderate (7:30 pace).
Tuesday—Speedwork.
Wednesday—6 miles moderate (7:30 pace).
Thursday—Speedwork.
Friday—5-6 miles moderate (7:30 pace).
Saturday—Road race or 4-mile run (7:00 pace).
Sunday—8 miles easy (7:45 pace).

Gawain Guy

GAWAIN GILBERT GUY   J. Frank Dobie High School

Born 1/28/62   Houston, Texas

5-9   135   Coach John Bryan

COMPETITIVE BACKGROUND
Gawain began competing at age 13 when Coach Bryan asked him to go out for track, and developed into a Texas State Champion and All-American in the 800 meters. Guy was the nation's No. 1 miler in 1981 and won the International Prep and Golden West miles.

BEST TIMES
48.7(m)   1:50.8(m)   3:51.72(1500m)   4:12.11

AGE GROUP MARKS

Year	Age	400	800	1500
1977	14	53.7		
1978	15	53.0		
1979	16		2:00	
1980	17		1:56.0	
1981	18	48.7	1:50.8	3:51.72

PREPARATION
Gawain uses a 2-mile warmup and a 2-mile warmdown before and after each practice. He does no special flexibility work and no weight training.

TRAINING COMMENTS
Gawain feels that the distance base he built during cross-country season was the most important part of his training; if he could "do it over again" he would run more mileage in the summer.

DAILY SEASONAL WORKOUTS

Fall
Cross Country.

Winter
January 28-February 3
Monday—6x880 on grass at 2:30 pace 880 jog between each.
Tuesday—5 miles on track at 6:30 pace.
Wednesday—40-minute fartlek run on grass.
Thursday—3000 meters on track.
Friday—7-mile run on roads.
Saturday—Rest.
Sunday—Rest.

Early Spring
March 17-March 23
Monday—8x300 (45 seconds) with a 150 jog between each.
Tuesday—7-mile run on roads.
Wednesday—2 sets of 440 (65 seconds); jog 55-440 (65 seconds); jog 880 between sets; 1x330.
Thursday—7-mile run on grass.
Friday—3-mile run on grass.
Saturday—Relay meet—1200 meter in distance medley(3:14), 4 x 800 leg(1:57), 4 x 400 leg (50.0).
Sunday—Rest.

Mid-Spring
April 7-April 13
Monday—6x880(2:20) with 3-minute jog between each.
Tuesday—5-mile run on grass.
Wednesday—8x300 (45 seconds) with 140 jog between each.
Thursday—5 laps, mile at 5:00, 5th lap all out.
Friday—3-mile run on grass.
Saturday—Invitational—800(1:58.0),   4 x 4 leg(50.9)—wet track.
Sunday—Rest

Gawain Guy

Late Spring-Championship Season
April 28-May 10

Monday—3x300(48) with 140 jog between each; 3x300(46) with 140 jog between each; 1x300(42); 1x300(41) jog 140 between each.

Tuesday—6-mile run on grass.

Wednesday—4x1320(3:30) with 880 jog between each.

Thursday—8-mile run on grass.

Friday—3-mile run on grass.

Saturday—Meet of Champions—800(1:51.7).

Sunday—Rest.

Monday—12x220 with first 4 in 34 seconds, next 8 in 30 seconds, jog 220 between each.

Tuesday—6-mile run on roads.

Wednesday—4x440 kick-ins.

Thursday—3 miles on track in 18:00—raining.

Friday—Travel to Austin; jog.

Saturday—State Meet—800(1:50.8).

Jim Haffner

JAMES PATRICK HAFFNER   Berea High School

Born 4/6/63   Berea, Ohio

5-10   140   Coach Harl Evans

COMPETITIVE BACKGROUND

Eventually his track team's captain and his school's most valuable cross-country and distance runner, Jim went out for track to follow a long family tradition of participating in track.

BEST TIMES

2:00.5(y)   4:20.3   9:34.5

AGE GROUP MARKS

Year	Age	880	Mile	2-Mile
1978	15		5:04	
1979	16		4:49	10:14
1980	17	2:04	4:25	9:42
1981	18	2:00.5	4:20.3	9:34.5

PREPARATION

Before practice, Jim warms up with a ½ mile jog and 15 minutes of stretching; before races he increases the jog to 2-3 miles, stretches, and tries to stay loose. While warming up alone, he goes over his race plan—preferring to go out slow and take the lead in the last lap. His typical mile race splits are 68-67-67-60.

TRAINING COMMENTS

Jim feels that his long distance workouts have been

most important, and given the chance to "do it over again," he would run more distance earlier in his career to develop a stronger base.

DAILY SEASONAL WORKOUTS

Winter
February 9-15
Monday—5-mile run.
Tuesday—8-mile run.
Wednesday—9-mile fartlek run.
Thursday—Rest.
Friday—11-mile run.
Saturday—6-mile run; 10x220 (35-36 seconds).
Sunday—4-mile run; 3x½ mile (2:26-2:30).

Spring
April 28-May 4
Monday—5-mile run; 8x110 (17 seconds).
Tuesday—Dual meet: 1 mile (4:23.9) and 880 (2:00.5).
Wednesday—5-mile run; 2x220; 4x110.
Thursday—2-mile run; 8x440 (64 seconds); 2 mile warmdown.
Friday—5-mile run.
Saturday—Relay meet: 1 mile (4:20.3) 1 mile (4:27) 880 (2:00.5).
Sunday—7-mile run.

Summer
June 30-July 6
Monday—9-mile run (AM). 6-mile run (PM).
Tuesday—7-mile run (AM). 7-mile run (PM).
Wednesday—6-mile run (AM). 2-mile run (PM).
Thursday—7-mile run (AM). 4-mile run (PM).
Friday—7-mile run (AM). 7-mile run (PM).
Saturday—7-mile run (AM). 6-mile run (PM).
Sunday—7-mile run (AM). 7-mile run (PM).

Fall

August 11-17

Monday—5-mile run (AM). 5- mile run (afternoon); 7-mile run (PM).

Tuesday—8-mile run; 4x½ miles on hills; 2½-mile warmdown, 3-mile run.

Wednesday—4½-mile run; 4x½ miles on hills; 2½-mile warmdown, 3-mile run.

Thursday—13-mile run.

Friday—5-mile run; 4x440 (62-64 seconds).

Saturday—5-mile run.

Sunday—3-mile run.

Tim Hacker

TIMOTHY A. HACKER   Menomonee Falls North HS

Born 12/27/62   Menomonee, Wisconsin

5-8   135   Coach Bob Rymer

COMPETITIVE BACKGROUND
Hacker is a two-time Wisconsin Cross-Country Champion and the International Prep 2-mile runner-up. Tim went out for track to follow in the footsteps of three older brothers. In 1981, he was an All-American at 3000 meters.

BEST TIMES
50.4(m)   1:53.86(m)   4:14.03   8:55.0   15:02(5k XC)

AGE GROUP MARKS
Year	Age	800	Mile	2-Mile	3-Mile XC
1978	15	2:12.2	4:35.8	10:09	15:40
1979	16	1:58.9	4:24.9	9:36.2	15:02
1980	17	1:54.9	4:19.6	9:18.0	14:53
1981	18	1:53.86	4:14.03	8:55.0	15:02(5k)

PREPARATION
Tim warms up before races with a long 1½-mile run, 20-30 minutes of "quality" stretching, and jogging, with sprints just before the race. He tries to work with weights 2-3 times each week during the season, doing his lifting on easy running days.

Bench Press   10 reps 125lb.   Curls   10 reps 40lb.

Military Press   10 reps   80lb.   Bar Dips   10-15 reps
Sit-ups   30 after every run   Push-ups   20-30 every day

TRAINING COMMENTS

Tim feels that outstanding coaching—the proper combination of distance, speed, and mental preparation—has been the most important part of his training.

"My fall workouts were 5k in 18-22 minutes every morning except Saturday, as well as afternoon team work. Our workouts were varied week-to-week; pick-ups would start at the beginning of the season at about 5 minutes easy, then 2 minutes hard, and 7 minutes easy. We do about four 2-minute runs with 7 minutes easy running between and a 5-10 minute run at the end. As the season progressed, the time on the beginning and end would be lengthened and the "rest" time between the 2-minute pick-ups would be shortened—another hard 2 minute run would be added for a total of five. The time between the pick-ups was called "easy," but was at a good 6:30-7:00 pace.

"Spring workouts varied depending on when the meets were. A "goal pace" workout was done at a goal you set for yourself—a 2-mile goal pace workout would be: 1 mile/3-4 minutes rest/880/2-3 minutes rest/440/rest equal to 440 time/2x220 with 1 minute rest between. Pick ups were used as in the fall, except not as often. We would do more track work and I continued my 5k morning runs.

"The summer before my freshmen year I ran 250 miles, the next summer 350, the next 450, and the short summer before my senior year, 500. I am not an advocate of high milage for high schoolers, and the most I've ever done was a little over 70 miles a week, and that was with two workouts a day during my senior year. I feel that for improvement each year, your base mileage—what you run in the summer and winter—should increase by a good amount each year. My winter mileage was similar quality mileage. Quality mileage is better [than simply long distances] for a high schooler.

"Running is much more a mental sport than most people think; to run well you must have a proper mental frame of mind, not only in races but everyday. If a high schooler runs too many miles, he gets tired of the sport and loses his mental edge or the sport no longer becomes enjoyable.

"My race tactics differ with each race. I'm a strong finisher, but I don't like to depend on my kick to win races. I try to run my splits even or increase the pace throughout the race. I'll lead if the pace is dragging, or sit back if it goes out too fast. I can adjust during the race, however most times I have a good idea how the race will go out and adjust accordingly so that my splits are even and I get the highest place possible."

DAILY SEASONAL WORKOUTS

Fall
Monday—5-7-mile run or small dual meet.
Tuesday—Pick-ups.
Wednesday—5-7-mile run.
Thursday—12x440 at pace or goal pace.
Friday—3-5 miles easy.
Saturday—Meet or hard workout of repeat miles at pace.
Sunday—5-7 miles.
5K run in 18-22 minutes each morning.

Winter
"I run once a day during the winter. I run a long hard run one day, a bit easier the next. There are no set workouts or speedwork of any kind during the winter; just good quality milage every day. During my senior year, as track approached, I went to twice-a-day workouts."

Spring
Monday—5-7 miles easy.
Tuesday—220s-330s-440s.
Wednesday—5-7 miles at medium pace.
Thursday—Repeat ½-mile pick-ups.
Friday—3-5 miles easy.
Saturday—Meet or 440s.
Sunday—5-7 miles easy.

Summer
Summer mileage averages 7 miles each day, with workouts varying so that some runs are long and slow and other are short and fast. The summer before senior year, workouts go to twice-a-day about a month before the fall season starts.

Ceci Hopp

CECILIA KIRSTEN HOPP   Greenwich High School

Born 4/13/63   Greenwich, Connecticut

5-5   105   Coaches Bill Mongovan
                                                  Garland Allen

COMPETITIVE BACKGROUND
Ceci went out for winter track as a sophomore to get in shape for tennis. She became the 1980 Kinney National Cross Country and National Junior 3000-meter Champion. Also voted Connecticut's Outstanding Amateur Athlete.

BEST TIMES
50(m)   2:13.06(m)   4:28(1500m)   4:45(1 mile)
9:21.02(3000m)   10:23(2 mile)   17:12(5k XC)

AGE GROUP MARKS

Year	Age	400	800	1500/Mile	3000/2-Mile
1979	15	61	2:19	4:58.7(1 mile)	11:40(2 mile)
1980	16	injured			9:47.9(3000m)
1981	17	59	2:13.06	4:23.3/4:42.6	9:21.0/10:23.3

PREPARATION
Ceci lifts weights on a non-regular basis and stays away from most junk food—except her favorite, ice cream—in order to keep her weight as low as possible without feeling weak.

Flexibility is very important to Ceci; she takes ballet once a week and stretches out twice a day, concentrating on her calves and hamstrings.

TRAINING COMMENTS

"My stretching and ballet background, along with the distance base I have been accumulating, are the most important parts of my training.

"In the fall of 1979 I had a successful cross country season, then went straight into indoor track with a lot of speed work and developed stress fractures. If I could do it over again I would mix the distance running more with my track workouts.

"During cross country I always went out in front from the beginning and concentrated on relaxing, saving energy, and staying there. In track I usually go out in front unless there is a rabbit. In my best mile (Girls Eastern Indoor Championships, Harvard University), I stayed on a girl's shoulder until the last 300 meters, then kicked by her. I concentrated on passing her especially fast to make it look like I had more energy than I really had.

"I've only been running a little over two years. What I am running now I could have never done as a sophomore. I have developed a lot more endurance and am putting in a lot more mileage. I have also done a lot of my training on my own—and I feel it is important to run how you feel; listen to your body. If something hurts, something is wrong and your body is telling you. Also, from freshmen to senior year, your body (especially girls') changes tremendously—you mature and gain weight and your body has to adjust to this. I think many girls have problems with this and become injured during their junior and senior years. I had stress fractures in both of my shins which led to a hip injury; it was a frustrating experience but it showed me how much I really love running."

DAILY SEASONAL WORKOUTS

Summer

"The beginning of summer is like spring, and is the most competitive season; the end is like fall with a lot of base-building and distance for cross country."

Fall

Monday—6-mile run; 1½-hour ballet class.

Tuesday—X-C meet—5000 meters; 3 miles after.
Wednesday—3-mile run (AM). 8-mile run (PM); swimming.
Thursday—4x2 miles (1st warmup, 2nd & 3rd at race pace, 4th warmdown).
Friday—6-mile run.
Saturday—3-mile run (AM). 5-mile run (PM).
Sunday—3-mile run (AM). Bicycling in afternoon.

Winter

"My weeks varied too much to record here; I did a lot more speed work, but also used this season to rest somewhat. I ran in competitive meets but did not concentrate on my training—especially mileage—as much."

Spring

Monday—7-mile run; 8x110 accelerations on grass; upper-body weightlifting; 1½-hour ballet class.
Tuesday—2-mile run (AM). Track meet—800, 1500, 3000 meters.
Wednesday—1-mile warmup; 4x100; 2x200; 2x400; 2x600; 1x800; 3-mile loop on golf course.
Thursday—2-mile run (AM). Swimming in afternoon; 7-mile run.
Friday—1-mile warmup; 4x100; 2x800 (2:20); 3-miles on golf course.
Saturday—3-mile run (AM). 9-mile run (PM).
Sunday—6-mile run on golf course (AM). Bicycling 6 miles in afternoon.

Kevin King

KEVIN GERALD-JOHN KING

Born 8/11/63

6-0   155

Westhill High School

Stamford, Connecticut

Coach Jim Hanneken

COMPETITIVE BACKGROUND
Kevin was the Connecticut indoor and outdoor State champion at 1500 meters and State recordholder at 1500 and 3000 meters. He began competing as a freshman, in cross-country. King was a prep All-American in the 1500 in 1981.

BEST TIMES
1:55.8(m)   3:55.2(1500m)   8:30.86(3000m)   14:50.78(5k)

AGE GROUP MARKS

Year	Age	800/880	1500/Mile	3000/2-Mile	5k
1978	14	2:14(y)	4:51(y)	10:04.8(y)	
1979	15	2:08(y)	4:27(y)	9:30.0(y)	
1980	16	1:56.3(m)	3:55.9(m)		
1981	17	1:55.8(m)	3:55.2(m)	8:30.86/9:11.2	14:50.78

PREPARATION
Kevin works out at a Nautilus center, doing one set of maximum repetitions at each machine. To warmup before practice and races, he alternates two 1-mile jogs with sessions of stretching.

TRAINING COMMENTS
Kevin feels that running intervals on trails is a very important part of his training, and if he could "do it again"

would stay off the track as much as possible and increase his trail workouts.

DAILY SEASONAL WORKOUTS

Fall
  Monday—3x1-mile on trail or roads.
  Tuesday—8-10-mile run—easy pace.
  Wednesday—3x1-mile, 880.
  Thursday—6-8-mile run—easy pace.
  Friday—6-8-mile run—easy pace.
  Saturday—Long fartlik run on trails.
  Sunday—6-8-mile run—easy pace.

Winter
  Monday—3x(440-800-440).
  Tuesday—6-10-mile run—easy pace.
  Wednesday—8x440.
  Thursday—6-8-mile run—easy pace.
  Friday—6x660.
  Saturday—5-6-mile run—easy pace.
  Sunday—4-5-mile run—easy pace.

Spring
  Monday—3x(660-440-660-220-440).
  Tuesday—6-10-mile run—easy pace.
  Wednesday—2x(660-440-220-220-440-660).
  Thursday—6-10-mile run—easy pace.
  Friday—6-8 hills very hard.
  Saturday—6-8 miles—easy pace.
  Sunday—4-5-mile run—easy pace.

Summer
  "This is time not to run. High school athletes have 12 years to run after leaving school—too many high school runners are overtraining, especially during the summer."

Patty Ley

PATRICIA ANN LEY   Gig Harbor High School

Born 4/2/65   Gig Harbor, Washington

5-4½   102   Coach Joel Wingard

COMPETITIVE BACKGROUND
An athletic, academic, and leadership award winner, Patty was also State division champion in cross country and in the 800- and 1600-meter runs. She gained her track interest by attending several small area meets while in elementary school. As a 7th grader, she began training with the high school team nearby.

BEST TIMES
50(r) 2:15.27(m) 4:28.5 4:58(1600m) 11:44.8(3200m)

AGE GROUP MARKS

Year	Age	400	800	1500	1600
1978	13	63	2:20		5:19
1979	14	62.2	2:20		5:18
1980	15	59	2:20	4:36.5	4:49.9
1981	16	58	2:15.27	4:28.5	4:58

PREPARATION
Patty works out with weights 2-3 times each week doing squats—leg extensions, leg curls, bench press, chin-ups, seated

press, lateral pull downs, dips, bicep curls, and sit-ups—going through 1-2 sets of 8-12 repetitions at 10-15 pounds below maximum. Chin-ups and dips are done to maximum, and 35-50 sit-ups are done each session.

One hour before races, Patty begins her warmup with a 20-25 minute easy run, then does her stretching, lightly at first then increasing intensity. Ten minutes before the race she runs 1-3x80-yard strides, checking to see if anything is tight; if so she stretches that muscle, if not she runs 2-3 more strides to finish loosening up.

TRAINING COMMENTS

Patty has enjoyed all of her training, but feels her hill training and distance work have been important in building strength and endurance.

DAILY SEASONAL WORKOUTS

Fall

Monday—20-minutes stretching, 15 minutes warmup; 7x880 at a good pace with 2 minute rest between each; 5x100 (2 bounding, 2 "butt kicks," 1 skipping); 1-mile warmdown; weight training; stretching.
Tuesday—20-minutes stretching; ladder run; 5x100 strides; stretching.
Wednesday—20-minutes stretching; 10x100 sprints, 3-mile run on course; weight training; stretching.
Thursday—Dual meet.
Friday—20-minutes stretching, 15-minute warmup; 10x300 shuttle relays; 20-minute warmdown; weight training, stretching.
Saturday—20-minute stretching; 60-75 minute run.
Sunday—Stretching—60 minute run. Monday-Friday Patty runs 20-40 minutes each morning.

Winter

Monday—7-10-mile run hard.
Tuesday—Easy-to-medium fartlek run.
Wednesday—7-10-mile run.

Thursday—Light interval speedwork.
Friday—7-10-mile run.
Saturday—Time trial, 3000-10,000 meters.
Sunday—7-12-mile run.

Spring

Monday—20-minute stretching, 3½-4 mile warmup; 5x80 strides; 4x800 with 4-5 minute rest interval; 8x200; 1½-2 mile warmdown.

Tuesday—20-minute stretching; 60-minute fartlek run including 2x200 strides, 6x50 sprints and 3-4 hill bounds; ballistic drills (bounding, skipping, butt kicks); weight training.

Wednesday—20-minutes stretching, 3½-4 mile warmup; 4x400; 10x150 sprints; 1½-2-mile warmdown.

Thursday—20-minutes stretching; 45 minute run; weight training

Friday—Dual meet—400 and mile relay.

Saturday—Invitational meet—1500 meters, 800 meters, mile relay

Sunday—60-minute run. Morning runs 3 days each week.

Summer

Monday—Intervals.
Tuesday—7-10-mile run.
Wednesday—Fartlek or hard 6-8-mile run.
Thursday—Light speed work.
Friday—5-8-mile run.
Saturday—Meet or road race.
Sunday—60-75-minute run.

Jay Marden

JAY DEE MARDEN Mission San Jose High School

Born 3/22/63 Fremont, California

6-0 158 Coach John Marden

COMPETITIVE BACKGROUND
Jay was a basketball player until a broken finger pointed the way to cross country. Jay won the Kinney National Championship and was named to the Adidas All-American Team. In 1981, Marden was No. 2 on the prep lists in the 3000, 2-mile, and steeplechase. He was 2nd in the State 3200 and a high school All-American.

BEST TIMES
4:11.9   8:54.75   9:24.7(St.)   8:17.7(3k)

AGE GROUP MARKS

Year	Age	Mile	2-Mile
1978	15	4:30.5	9:35.8
1979	16	4:19.3	9:11.9
1980	17	4:14.6	8:59.22
1981	18	4:11.9	8:54.75

PREPARATION
Jay does a great deal of overall stretching and warmups with 4-6 laps, stretching, and 6-10 hard 100-yard build-ups. He works with weights three days each week;

| Bench Press | 3x10 | Military Press | 3x10 |
| Curls | 3x10 | Upright Row | 3x10 |

TRAINING COMMENTS

Jay feels that short interval 220s and 440s have been the most important part of his training. "Maybe I could have had longer off-season runs, but I'm saving some work for college," he adds.

Jay likes to know his competition. He prepares his mind to run with anybody, but keeps his own strategy of going out hard to break the competition. He agrees with his dad who is also his coach that "anyone you can run with, you can beat."

DAILY SEASONAL WORKOUTS

Fall
Monday—8-10-mile hilly run.
Tuesday—Interval work—10 short sprints; 6x600 on course.
Wednesday—Speed-play, or 40 minutes of light intervals.
Thursday—League race—use as a hard workout.
Friday—10 short sprints; 8x220, with 220 jog between each.
Saturday—Invitational.
Sunday—10-mile run.

Winter
Run 6-10 miles each day with the Polar Bear Club; no interval training; rest from racing except for competitive fun runs.

Spring
Monday—Interval day-8-10x330-440, pace depends on progress etc.; hard sprints at end.
Tuesday—Intervals stressing strength and endurance—660s and 880s.
Wednesday—Easy speed-play; 10xshort sprint build-ups; 6x220 build-ups.
Thursday—Competition—stress speed.
Friday—Easy speed play.
Saturday—Competition.
Sunday—10-mile run.

Summer
Summer Mileage Club: run 6-11 miles each day, run in road races for fun only.

Patty
Matava

PATRICIA ANN MATAVA	Bellevue High School
Born 10/8/65	Bellevue, Washington
5-3 90	Coach R. Nolan

COMPETITIVE BACKGROUND

Patty began running in junior high school because it seemed easy and other members of her family were also involved in running. She became Washington State Champion in cross country and the 3200-meter run, and led the nation in the 2-mile in 1981.

BEST TIMES

2:20(m)   4:28.5   4:48.9(1600m)   9:27.3(3000m) 10.09(3200m)

AGE GROUP MARKS

Year	Age	800	1500	1600	3000	3200
1978	12	2:47				
1979	13			5:31		
1980	14		4:38	5:10	9:44.22	
1981	15	2:20	4:28.5	4:48.9	9:27.3	10:09

PREPARATION

During the off season Patty works with weights 3-4 days each week:

Toe Lifts	2x25	16lb.	Step-ups	2x30	16lb.
Bench Press	2x20	16lb.	Clean & Press	2x15	16lb.

Curls	2x15	16lb.	Bentover Row	2x20	16lb.
Squats	100	25lb.	Leg Curls	3x10	10lb.
Sit-ups	3x25				

One half hour before races, Patty jogs 2-3 laps, stretches for 15 minutes, runs 4x100 pickups, then continues to stretch until the gun.

TRAINING COMMENTS

Mentally, Patty prepares for a race by being totally familiar with the locale—noting all of the holes, turns, and hills on a cross-country course and knowing tracks well enough to run the race several times in her head before the actual race. She enjoys going on long runs while running hills is her least favorite workout. Patty feels that running year 'round has been the most important part of her training.

DAILY SEASONAL WORKOUTS

Fall

Monday—10x440 (1st 5 paced, 2nd 5 fast); 30-minute run at medium pace.

Tuesday—1-hour run.

Wednesday—Run hills for 30 minutes; 30-minute run at easy to medium pace.

Thursday—Pace work—2-3x440; 4x110 strides; easy 30-minute run.

Friday—Competition.

Saturday—6-8-mile run at easy to medium pace.

Sunday—8-mile run at medium hard pace.

Winter

Monday—Mile run at hard pace; weight training.

Tuesday—8-mile run at medium-hard pace.

Wednesday—8-mile run at medium-hard pace; weight training.

Thursday—8-mile run at medium hard pace.

Friday—8-mile run at medium hard pace; weight training.

Saturday—3-mile easy run; or 8-mile run and weight

training.
Sunday—Road race; or 8-mile run and weight training.

Spring

Monday—10x440; or 6x880; or 6-10x220; and 30 minute run.
Tuesday—1-hour run.
Wednesday—15 minutes of hill running, 6x220 paced; 20-30-minute run.
Thursday—2-3x440 paced; 30-minute run at easy pace.
Friday—Competition.
Saturday—6-8-mile run at easy pace.
Sunday—8-mile run at medium-hard pace.

Summer

Monday—8-mile run at hard pace, during the last mile surge for 50 yards several times, then return to pace.
Tuesday—1x550; 3x220; 1x550; 3-4x165; 20-minute run at easy pace.
Wednesday—8-mile run at medium-hard pace with several surges in final 880.
Thursday—4x440; 3-4x165; 20-30-minute run at easy pace.
Friday—4-mile run at easy pace with surges during final 880.
Saturday—Competition.
Sunday—8-10-mile run at enjoyable pace.

George Nicholas

GEORGE NICK NICHOLAS   Meadowdale High School

Born 7/9/63   Dayton, Ohio

6-0   140   Coaches Steve Schoemann
Steve Price

COMPETITIVE BACKGROUND

A fourth-place finish in the IAAF Junior International Cross Country Championships highlights an outstanding running career which includes 3 Ohio Cross-Country Championships and national age-group championships in cross country, 1500, and 3000 meters.

BEST TIMES

1:55.7(m)   3:53.0   8:18.5
11:36.8(2½-Mile XC)   66:09(½-marathon)

AGE GROUP MARKS

Year	Age	800	1500	3000	2½-Mile XC
1978	14	2:03	4:05	8:53	12:28
1979	15	1:59.5	3:59	8:27	11:45
1980	16	injured			11:50
1981	17	1:55.7	3:53	8:18.5	11:36.8

DAILY SEASONAL WORKOUTS

Fall

Monday—5 miles in 29:30(AM). 2-mile warmup, 16x330

(50 seconds), 4x110 uphill, 1-mile jog (PM).
Tuesday—5 miles in 34:30 (AM). 6 miles in 42:00, 3 miles in 15:00, 1-mile jog (PM).
Wednesday—3-mile warmup; 4x1 mile (4:52, 4:52, 4:48, 4:42) with 880 jog recovery, 1 mile jog (PM).
Thursday—5 miles in 29:30 (AM).8 miles in 50:00 (PM).
Friday—8 miles in 56:00 (PM).
Saturday—Race—2½ miles in 11:49.

Sunday—12 miles in 82:00.
All fall training is done in a park.

Winter

Monday—8 miles in 55:00 (AM). 2-mile warmup; 4x220 (30 seconds), 8x440 (61 seconds) with 440 jog recovery, 3x220 (33-30-27), 1-mile jog (PM).
Tuesday—12 miles in 82:00 (PM).
Wednesday—8 miles in 55:00 (AM). 3-mile warmup, 4x440 (58-59-59-58) with 440 jog recovery, 1-mile jog (PM).
Thursday—4 miles easy (PM).
Friday—Race—3-mile warmup, mile in 4:12, 2-mile jog, 880 in 1:58.
Saturday—Rest.
Sunday—12 miles in 82:00.

Spring

Monday—3-mile warmup; 6x330 (42-43) with 220 jog recovery, 1 mile jog.
Tuesday—8 miles in 54:00.
Wednesday—3-mile warmup; 6x660 (1:32) with 440 jog recovery, 880 jog, 4x110 (14) 1-mile jog.
Thursday—4 miles easy.
Friday—Race—Mile in 4:19, 30 minute rest, 880 in 1:55.7, 1-mile jog, 2-mile in 9:26.
Saturday—10-mile fartlek run with 4x880 and 4x440 and 68 quarter pace.
Sunday—8 miles in 45:20.

Summer

Monday—3-mile warmup, 6x440 (58 seconds) with 220 jog recovery, 1-mile jog.
Tuesday—4 miles easy.
Wednesday—3-mile warmup; 4 x880 (2:02-2:04) with 440 jog recovery, 1-mile jog.
Thursday—6 miles in 34:00.
Friday—4 miles easy.
Saturday—Race—1-mile in 4:14, 2-mile in 9:00.6.
Sunday—8 miles in 53:20.

Brian Pettingill

BRIAN ROGER PETTINGILL   Cheverus High School

Born 7/12/63   Portland, Maine

5-11   138   Coach Charles Malia

COMPETITIVE BACKGROUND
Eventually Maine's finest prep distance runner, Brian went out for track as a 12-year-old because it was a "different, non-traditional" sport. A track All-American and National Honor Society member, he holds State records in the 600, 880, 1000, and mile.

BEST TIMES
49.0(y, r)   1:50.9(m)   4:10.0   14:13(5k XC)

AGE GROUP MARKS

Year	Age	Mile	880
1977	13	4:38	2:05
1978	14	4:22	2:00
1979	15	4:15	1:57
1980	16	4:10	1:51.8(m, r)
1981	17	4:11.8(i)	1:50.9(m)

PREPARATION
Brian has been pleased with his high school training and says he "wouldn't change a thing." He lifts weights every other day on a Universal Machine (Bench Press 3x10 130#, Military Press 3x10 100#, Curls 3x10 70#). Before a distance workout Brian warms up with a lot of "stretching;"

before speed work he stretches and adds a 2-3 mile run. He eats a regular diet during the season and carbohydrate-loads two nights before a meet.

TRAINING COMMENTS

Pettingill enjoys short speed work—220s and 440s—and lists them as his favorite workout, but feels that long fast 1-and 2-mile loops have been most important.

Before racing, Brian puts himself in a positive attitude and tries to mentally put himself through the race to get his adrenalin going. Early in his career he was hurt by a lack of local competition and was forced to set the pace for fast times. Traveling to big meets has allowed Brian to sit on the pace and use his speed for a big kick finish.

DAILY SEASONAL WORKOUTS

Fall

Monday—1-mile warmup; 4x1-mile(4:45) with 4 minute rest interval; 1-mile warmdown.

Tuesday—7 miles easy (7:00 pace).

Wednesday—1-mile warmup; 2x5000 meters in 15 minutes and 18 minutes with a 20 minute rest interval; 1-mile warmdown.

Thursday—8 miles moderate (6:15 pace).

Friday—1-mile warmup; 880 (2:00); 1320 (3:20); 1-mile (4:20); 2-mile (9:20); 1-mile warmdown.

Saturday—7 miles easy (7:00 pace).

Sunday—7 miles moderate fast (6:15-5:45 pace).

Winter

Monday—3½-mile warmup; 4x880 (2:15) 1-mile warm down.

Tuesday—5 easy miles with middle two at 5:00 pace.

Wednesday—3-mile warmup; 110-220-110-2 11-330-110-330; 110-440-110-440; 110-550-110-550; 880 (2:25); 880 warmdown.

Thursday—2-mile warmup; 220-440-660-440-220-440; 880

warmdown.
Friday—Stretching and striding, 3 miles.
Saturday—Competition.
Sunday—4 miles easy.

Spring

Monday—4-mile warmup; 12x220 fast with a 110 jog interval; 880 warmdown.
Tuesday — 1 - mile warmup (6:00); 6x880 (2:10-2:00-2:10-2:00-2:30-2:00) with a 10-minute rest interval; 1-mile warmdown.
Wednesday—2½-mile warmup; 5-mile run with the first three miles in 15:00; 2½-mile warmdown.
Thursday—1-mile warmup; 3 sets 8x110 continuous pick-ups; 1-mile warmdown.
Friday—4 miles easy with 6x80 yard pick-ups in the middle.
Saturday—Competition.
Sunday—8 miles easy.

Summer

"I usually use the summer just to relax and run some long slow distance to build a base back up for the competitive season."

Rickey Pittman

RICKEY L. PITTMAN   East Tech High School

Born 10/4/61   Cleveland, Ohio

5-10   140   Coach James A. Emery

COMPETITIVE BACKGROUND
Rickey went out for track in junior high school to prove to his friends that he could be successful at a sport. Successful he was, being twice named to prep all-american teams. Rickey was also International Prep 2-mile champion, and ran 1980's fastest prep 2-mile.

BEST TIMES
4:10.6   8:49.4   30:12.6(10k)   46:19(15k roads)

AGE GROUP MARKS

Year	Age	880	Mile	2-Mile	2.5-Mile XC
1977	15	2:06.0	4:42.0		
1978	16		4:17.1	9:28.1	
1979	17	1:58.6(r)	4:21.9	9:38	12:13 injured
1980	18	1:56.0(r)	4:10.7	8:49.4	11:44

PREPARATION
Rickey did light upper body weight lifting twice each week from late fall to early spring.

TRAINING COMMENTS
Pittman feels that establishing a good mileage base over the summer and winter, and good hard track workouts to

improve racing ability, were the most important parts of his training.

"For race tactics, I try to break the competitors before the last lap, particularly during the middle ¾ of the race. This makes it mentally tough on my opponents, since they will have to run hard when they really want to rest for their finishing kicks."

FROM COACH EMERY

One aspect of Rickey's training which helped with his development was hard intensity track work during the season (both cross-country and track, but particularly the latter). Much of this was designed to improve his strength, but also to develop racing tactics. Varied paces were emphasized by altering workout paces and not announcing the pace to be run until three seconds before an interval was to begin. Also, intervals for rest were consistently cut throughout the season."

"Of course, like any distance runner, the biggest 'secret' to his success was Rickey's personal motivation."

DAILY SEASONAL WORKOUTS

Fall
Monday—7-mile run at 6:00 pace (AM). 20x440 at 66 second pace with 220 jog between each (PM).
Tuesday—5-mile run-easy (AM). Dual meet—race easy or 8-mile run at 5:40 pace (PM).
Wednesday—7-mile run at 6:00 pace (AM). 4x1-mile at 4:28-4:35 pace (PM).
Thursday—5-mile run—easy (AM). 8-mile run at 6:30 pace; or 6x300 yard hill (PM).
Friday—5-mile run at 6:00 pace (AM). Pre-meet jogging and stretching (PM).
Saturday—Competition.
Sunday—12-20-mile run at "no-pressure pace."

Winter
Monday—7-mile run—easy (AM). 3 miles at 6:30 pace; 8x330 on steep hill, 3 miles at 6:00 pace (PM).
Tuesday—7-mile run at 6:00 pace (AM). Dual meet—2-mile

relay—1 mile—2 mile—880—jog continuously after each (PM).

Wednesday—5-mile run at 6:00 pace (AM). 12-mile run (PM).

Thursday—8-mile run at 6:30 pace (AM). 440 (65 seconds), jog 550, 660 (1:40), jog 770, 880 (2:16), jog 990, 110 (2:53), jog 1210, 1320 (3:30), then run ladder back down (PM).

Friday—5-mile-run—easy (AM). 6-10-mile run at 5:40-6:30 pace (PM).

Saturday—8-mile run at 6:00 pace or occasional race.

Sunday—16-20-mile run at "no pressure" pace.

Spring

Monday—7-mile run—easy (AM). 1½ miles at 6:55 pace; 880 jog; 1-mile (4:35); 880 jog; 1320 (3:20), 660 jog; 880 (2:08), 440 jog; 440 (58) (PM).

Tuesday—5-mile run at 6:30 pace (AM). 10-mile run at 6:15 pace (PM).

Wednesday—7-mile run—easy (AM). 10x440 (58) with 80-yard walk and 140 jog between each (PM).

Thursday—5-mile run at 6:30 pace (AM). 7-mile run at 6:00 pace; or 8x330 (43-45) (PM).

Friday—5-mile run—very easy (AM). Pre-meet jog and stretch (PM).

Saturday—Competition.

Sunday—8-14-mile run at "no-pressure" pace.

Summer

Monday—5-mile run—easy (AM). 10-mile run at 5:50 pace (PM).

Tuesday—7-mile run at 6:30 pace (AM). 4x1 mile (4:40) with 440 jog between each (PM).

Wednesday—5-mile run—easy (AM). 12-mile run over varied terrain at 6:00 pace (PM).

Thursday—7-mile run at 5:50 pace (AM). 3-mile run—easy; 8x660 on steep hill; 3-mile run—easy (PM).

Friday—5-mile run—easy (AM). 8-10-mile run (PM).

Saturday—7-10-mile fartlek run with 200-800 yard strides at 60%-90%; or 10k road race.

Sunday—16-20-mile run no faster than 6:00 pace.

Jessica Spies

JESSICA ANN SPIES   Livermore High School

Born 7/29/64   Livermore, California

5-5   112   Coach Augie Argabright

COMPETITIVE BACKGROUND

A 4.0 student, Jessica has won honors athletically, as well, taking the California North Coast Section 400 and 800, 2nd in the Cal State Meet 800, Junior Olympic Nationals 800, and Bruce Jenner High School 800. Jessica was also a member of the San Jose Cindergals 2-mile relay team which finished 3rd at the TAC nationals. In 1981, Jessica won prep All-American honors.

BEST TIMES

25.6(m)   55.6(m)   2:05.84   4:37.5(1500m)
10:01.2(3000m)

AGE GROUP MARKS

Year	Age	200	400	800	1500/Mile	3000
1979	14	25.8	59.0			
1980	15	25.6	55.3	2:11.8	5:36	
1981	16	25.6	56.4	2:05.84	4:37.5	10:01.2

PREPARATION

Jessica warms up with a 1-mile jog, 6x60-yard runs, and 5-10 minutes of stretching.

TRAINING COMMENTS

Spies states that "fantasic coaching" by Augie

Argabright has been the most important part of her training program, and, given the chance, she would make no changes. She tries to think positively about upcoming races and uses whatever tactics the race demands.

DAILY SEASONAL WORKOUTS

Fall

October

Monday—3-mile run and 6x60-yard warmup; 3x3-minute run on grass with a 15-second sprint at the end of each—60 second rest between each; 10x110; 7x3-minute run with 15-second sprint—60 second rest between each; 4x330; 110 sprint; 1x50-meter sprint.

Tuesday—1-mile warmup; 6x220; 5-mile hilly run.

Wednesday—6-mile run.

Thursday—1-mile and 6x60 warmup; 10x440 (1:40) with 20-second rest between each; jog 880; all-out 1100 meter run; 6x440 (2:00) with 20-second rest between each; jog 880; all-out 660-yard run; 1-mile warmdown with 50-yard sprint at the end of each lap.

Friday—3-mile run.

Saturday—5000 meter cross country race.

Sunday—5-mile run.

Winter

January

Monday—1-mile and 6x60 warmup; 12x30-second sprints with 30-second rest between each; jog 1-mile; walk 440; 8x30-second sprints with 30-second rest between each; 1-mile warmdown with 50-yard sprint at the end of each lap.

Tuesday—Run in park—2-mile and 6x60 warmup; 5x500 all-out with 200-walk recovery between each; jog 1-mile; 8x110 hill sprints.

Wednesday—1-mile and 6x60 warmup; 6x165 with 110 walk recovery; 6x440 (1:40) with 29 seconds rest between each; 4x165; jog 3 laps; relay 110s for 8 minutes (about 10x110); 6x40; 1-mile warmdown.

Thursday—Run in park—2-mile and 4x60 warmup; 4x110; all-out; jog 1-mile; 5x110 hill sprints.

Friday—1-mile and 6x60 warmup; all-out 5000-meter run; 4x110; 4x200; 4x110—walk same distance for recovery; 1-mile warmdown.

Saturday—All-comers meet.

Sunday—3.5-mile road race.

Spring
April
Sunday—1-mile and 6x60 warmup; 12-minute run; 4x220 relay; 10x440 on grass; 4x220 with 220 walk recovery; 4x50; 1-mile warmdown.

Monday—1-mile and 6x60 warmup; 1¼-mile all-out; jog 1-mile; all-out 1100 meters; jog 3 laps; all-out 330; jog 2 laps; 1x220; 10x200 accelerations (walk 50-jog 100-sprint 50); 1-mile warmdown.

Tuesday—1-mile and 6x60 warmup; 3-minute 880 with 440 kick; 3-minute 880 with 330 kick; 3-minute 880 with 220 kick; 3-minute 880 with 110 kick; jog 3 miles; 2x50 sprints.

Wednesday—1-mile warmup; 440 relay passes; 1-mile warmdown.

Thursday—Dual meet—440 relay-220-mile relay.

Friday—Bruce Jenner Classic—800-1500-mile relay.

Saturday—Rest.

Summer
July-August
"I try to average 50-70 miles a week with one 70-mile week. I go to all-comers meets occasionally and run odd events."

Stacey Zartler

STACEY ANN ZARTLER

Born 10/4/66

5-1   93

MacArthur High School

Metroplex Striders

Irving, Texas
Coach Terry Jessup

COMPETITIVE BACKGROUND
Stacey's soccer coach, seeing her running talent, suggested she try track: "I did and I loved it," as a 7-year-old, says Stacey. She has been in training seriously since she was 12, and is a national age-group champion.

BEST TIMES
57.8(m)   2:08.84(m)   4:31.45(1500m)

AGE GROUP MARKS

Year	Age	800	1500
1979	12	2:15.4	
1980	13	2:11.4	
1981	14	2:07.49	4:31.45

PREPARATION
Stacey warms up with 15 minutes of stretching, an easy mile run, and several stride runs. She tries to relax before races, thinking about strategy and times a few days before.

TRAINING COMMENTS
"Almost all of the training I do is based upon Arthur

Lydiard and his styles and methods of training.

For about 6 weeks in the fall, I work on running mileage and getting strength. I spend about 6 more weeks on sharpening skills. During the sharpening period, I do things like 4 miles fast at 5:50-6:00 with a mile jog between each. I also do 8x800 meters around 2:30-2:40.

"In early December I start working on conditioning. I do this for 2 months, trying to build a good base for the coming track season. I run many road races and try to run as many miles as possible.

"During February, I work on strength and prepare for the fast pace of the track season. I do this with drills like bounding and bouncing. I mix these drills with striding and sprinting up a 300-meter hill. I do wind sprints and intervals after every 10 minutes of hill work. This is done 3 days each week, on the other days I run 8-14 miles. I also compete in some indoor meets at this time.

"Next, I move to track—my favorite part of training. I work on building my anaerobic capacity for about 4 weeks, doing sprints and intervals 4 days each week and easy running on the other days. I spend about 4 weeks on coordination training, doing fast, short sprints, relaxed striding, and easy running with some fartlek work. I work on the track through July, then start training again for cross country."

DAILY SEASONAL WORKOUTS
Fall
Monday—Steady 9-14-mile run at 7:10 pace.
Tuesday—Relaxed 8-mile run at 7:15 pace.
Wednesday—Fast 10-12-mile run at 7:15 pace.
Thursday—6-8-mile fartlek run on hills.
Friday—Rest.
Saturday—Race, with extra running, 8-miles total.
Sunday—Easy 11-14-mile run.

Winter
Monday—Easy 6-8-mile fartlek run.
Tuesday—Fast 10-12 miles at sub-7:00 pace.
Wednesday—Easy 6-8-mile run.
Thursday—Fast 10-13-mile run at 6:45 pace.
Friday—Rest.

Saturday—Long time-trial or race, total mileage of 10-12 miles including extra running.
Sunday—Easy 11-16-mile run at 7:15-7:20 pace. During the winter, there are some morning runs of 3-5 miles.

Spring

Monday—Easy 8-mile run at 7:20 pace.
Tuesday—7 hills and intervals, 10 miles total.
Wednesday—Easy 6 miles of fartlek.
Thursday—7 hills and intervals, 10 miles total.
Friday—Rest.
Saturday—7 hills and intervals, 10 miles total.
Sunday—Steady 13-15-mile run.
There are some morning runs of 4 miles.

Summer

Monday—Speed intervals: 600 in 1:38, 200s under 30 seconds, 800 pickup in 2:16.
Tuesday—Aerobic training and strides or volume intervals.
Wednesday—Speedwork: 200s, 300s, 400s, or strength work.
Thursday—Easy 6-8-mile run at 7:20 pace.
Friday—Rest.
Saturday—Race.
Sunday—Easy 12-14-mile run at 7:15-7:20 pace.

John Zishka

JOHN LOUIS ZISHKA

Born 5/16/62

5-10   135

Lancaster High School

Lancaster, Ohio

Coaches Robert Reall
Terry Oehrtman

COMPETITIVE BACKGROUND

Eventually the Ohio State champion in cross country, the mile and 2-mile, John began competing as a 13-year-old "because everyone else was." In 1980, he led the U.S. in the mile, 3000, 5000, and was twice an All-American.

BEST TIMES

1:52.5(m)   4:03.85   8:13.9(3000m)   8:51.9   13:55(5k)

AGE GROUP MARKS

Year	Age	800	1320	Mile	3000/2-Mile	5k
1975	13		3:36			
1976	14	2:06	3:29	4:42		
1977	15	2:00.1		4:24		
1978	16			4:15	9:17(2m)	
1979	17	1:53.3(r)		4:08.5	8:51.9(2m)	14:11.2
1980	18	1:52.5(r)		4:03.8	8:13.9(3000m)	13:55.6

PREPARATION

John works with weights during the winter and summer. Using free weights he works on the bench press, curls, military press, and upright rowing—2-3 sets of 8 to 10 repetitions.

Before practice and meets, he warms up with jogging, stretching, and 150-yard pick-ups. He does nothing special to

psych-up, believing that it "is something that should come naturally . . . there really isn't anything special to do to get the adrenalin pumping."

TRAINING COMMENTS

"We rarely do any speed work during the fall; the shortest we would run might be 600 yards. Coach Reall stresses strength-work over speedwork. We have some pretty fast guys on the cross country team, so we basically got our speed work in races.

"During the winter, Coach Terry Oehrtman takes over the distance runners for track. We use a good combination of steady distance running during the winter to build a base for spring. He combines the best of both Lydiard training and some of the things he learned at Bowling Green University. Plus, we kind of experiment a little and found, I think, the best possible way for a runner to train. During the winter, Coch Oehrtman stresses overdistance, stretching, and weight training with equal importance.

"In late spring we start getting down to the nitty-gritty, trying to get sharp for the big meets. Our workouts might look like this:

a) Run a 330 pretty much all-out, with a little 110 jog around the curve to start the next 330. This would be repeated 3 or 4 times.

b) Run a 330 under 40 seconds, then jog a 110 and hit the back stretch in an all-out 110 concentrating on lift. Repeat 3 times.

c) Run 5-6x220 under 25 seconds with a 220 jog between each.

"Summer was really a time to rest. I usually don't race too far into the summer—never past July, because a high school kid shouldn't be running all the time. . .running should be fun. In the middle of the summer I start to get ready for fall cross country, going an easy 10 miles a day."

DAILY SEASONAL WORKOUTS
Fall

Monday—Fartlek run—5 miles at a steady sub-6:00 pace with 110 pick-ups under 5:30 pace; then running the same 5 miles, but the pick-ups become 440 surges.

Tuesday—Dual meet; steady run after meet.
Wednesday—Pace-work, running repeat mile intervals at race pace; or running a 2-5 mile workout trying to hit certain splits for each mile.
Thursday—8-10x200-yard hill runs, followed by a 5-mile run.
Friday—Easy 5-6-mile run followed by several strides.
Saturday—Competition; followed by a warmdown run of up to 5 miles.
Sunday—10-12-mile run.

Winter

"Winter is kind of nasty in Ohio and we have to run outdoors. We ran up to 10 miles each day, plus weight training and stretching. During late winter and early spring—if the track was clear—we run 6-8x150 strides after distance runs. We have a few low key indoor meets for a little speedwork and to break the boredom of overdistance training."

Spring

Monday—3x1500 on grass or 1x3000 and 2x1500.
Tuesday—Dual meet—run a pace workout before the meet of 4x880; or 8x440 at a bit faster than 1-mile pace.
Wednesday—Overdistance.
Thursday—2-3 ladders of 440 (brisk)-330 (good 70 second quarter pace)-220 (easy)-110 (hard)-220 (jog recovery).
Friday—5-mile run, followed by 150 pick-ups.
Saturday—Competition, usually 2-3 events.
Sunday—12-mile run.

Early Summer

Monday—Overdistance, followed by 150 pick-ups and weight training.
Tuesday—Overdistance; 150 pick-ups.
Wednesday—4x880; or 8x440; or 3x1320.
Thursday—3 ladders, 440-330-220-110-220.
Friday—Competition.
Saturday—Competition.
Sunday—Overdistance.

SPRINTERS/
MIDDLE DISTANCE

Anthony Ketchum

ANTHONY RAYE KETCHUM   Needville High School

Born 11/20/62   Needville, Texas

5-8   152   Coach Quinn Euby (78-80)
Coach Jack Petty ('81)

COMPETITIVE BACKGROUND

Anthony became interested in track while in elementary school and first competed as a 9-year-old in a summer track program. He is a two-time All American and National High School Record holder. His 45.5 Cal State Meet win is the second-fastest all-time.

BEST TIMES

10.47   20.8(m)   45.50(m)   1:52.03(m)

AGE GROUP MARKS

Year	Age	100	200	400	800
1978	15			47.5	
1979	16			47.3	
1980	17		21.0	46.8	
1981	18	10.47	20.8	45.5	1:52.03

PREPARATION

Anthony warms up with an 880-mile jog and 15-30 minutes of stretching before practice and meets. He likes to go off alone, sit, stretch, and think about his competition before meets—then go out and run his own race.

TRAINING COMMENTS

From Coach Jack Petty:

"What we did:

"Build as much base as possible; i.e., 20x200 at ¼-effort, 12x400s in early-season (January). This is fairly basic work. In the base work I don't like a lot of track work early. Other than for smoothness and speedwork, the track was designed for spectators, not the natural terrain of relaxed running. We avoided the track at other times when feasible to do so. I also dislike the use of weights during the season for must runners.

"The coaching aspect and decisions on the athlete's progress, as to when to attempt something, cannot be stressed too much. The coach must decide. We are all unique and will use somewhat differing techniques and methods, but the coach must adapt what he/she utilizes for the athlete at hand.

"Our speedwork training was never taxing in volume. We used the hard-easy approach. Speed was considered hard, no matter how little was scheduled. The same for meet days. Also incorporated was the Andrews program of Coach Max Goldsmith that put Ted Nelson at 46.5 twenty years earlier. This involved the gradual lowering of sprint times once we achieved a week's goal.

"Follow your plan. If you make changes, let it be from your own analysis and decision...Refuse to listen to arm-chair quarterbacks who know little of what is involved. I rested Anthony from a meet scheduled 10 days prior to District despite protests about it. When I entered him in the 800 meters the week prior to State there were criticisms drawn. Still, we knew the reasons for running the 800:

1. It removed any pressure of running 'the race' too early or feeling down if he didn't run hard enough in the 400.
2. It gives one a new perspective towards the 400, as practiced by Bill Toomey and Lee Evans. One distance complements the other.
3. Less chance of injury in the 800 than the sprints."

"The week before State we only did strides and worked on long jump steps.

"I have wondered, too, if Anthony might have done better had we taken another approach—say ran the 400 in the

Champions meet, etc. I asked him and we discussed it many times. He feels the sprints helped him approach the 45.5 by State and the 800 race definitely convinced him that he was strong enough to do it."

DAILY SEASONAL WORKOUTS
Mid-January
Monday—20x200 at ¼-effort.
Tuesday—40 minutes on roads.
Wednesday—10-12x400 at ¼-effort.
Thursday—12x300 at ¼-effort.
Friday—30-45-minute run on roads.
Saturday—Rest.
Sunday—Rest.

Mid-February
Monday—8x200 at ½-effort.
Tuesday—40 minutes of X-C.
Wednesday—3x500 at ¼-effort; 3x200 at ¼-effort.
Thursday—20x100-meter accelerations.
Friday—30-minute jog.
Saturday—Rest.
Sunday—Rest.

Mid-March
Monday—2x500 at ½-effort; 2x200 at ½-effort; or 2x(500-300-300-150).
Tuesday—5x200 at ¾-speed.
Wednesday—6x150 at ½-speed, relay work.
Thursday—6 starts; stride 6x100.
Friday—Jog.
Saturday—Competition.
Sunday—Rest.

Mid-April
Monday—2x(500-600-200) at ½-speed.
Tuesday—300-200-200-150 at ¾-speed.
Wednesday—2x200; 2x150 at ½-and ¾-speed.
Thursday—Starts; relay work.
Friday—Rest.
Saturday—Competition.
Sunday—Rest.

Mid-May
   Monday—2x200 at 7/8-speed.
   Tuesday—6 starts; 3x150.
   Wednesday—Strides; 1x500 at ½-speed.
   Thursday—Strides.
   Friday—Rest.
   Saturday—Competition—800 meters in 1:52.03.

Erik Modine

ERIK ALAN MODINE   Westchester High School

Born 6/14/63   Houston, Texas

6-2   170   Coach Chester Vlasek

COMPETITIVE BACKGOUND
Erik first went out for track in junior high, at age 14. He was voted the MVP of the Westchester Track Team as a senior.

BEST TIMES
48.7(y)   1:57(y)   15.2(HH)   38.1(330IH)

AGE GROUP MARKS

Year	Age	440	880	110HH	330IH
1978	14	55	2:07		
1979	15	51.9	2:04	15.9	40.9
1980	16	48.9	2:04	15.2	39.4
1981	17	48.7	1:57		38.1

PREPARATION
Erik worked with weights three days each week.

| Bench Press | 3x6 | Military Press | 3x6 |
| Lateral Pulls | 3x6 | Hamstring Pulls | 3x10 |

All lifts done at maximum weight.

He warms up for races with a 1-mile jog, stretching and 100-yard sprints, "to get quickness in the legs."

TRAINING COMMENTS

Repeating workouts and being pushed to run harder are the most important parts of Erik's training. He would, however, add more long distance work if he could "do it over again."

Coach Vlasek adds that "all speed work during the actual track season is always done in groups. At times, for a change of pace, we do 'endless relays' with 200-or 400-meter legs bo break the day-in-day-out monotony."

DAILY SEASONAL WORKOUTS

Fall
Monday—6-mile run at 6:00 pace.
Tuesday—4-mile run; 3x400 meters (65 seconds) with 3-minute rest between each; grass straightaways; 3x200 (30 seconds); grass straightaways.
Wednesday—6-mile hilly run.
Thursday—5-mile run; 3x400 (65 seconds); grass straightaways.
Friday—2-3 easy miles.
Saturday—Competition.
Sunday—6-mile easy run.

Winter
Monday—Weight training, 2-3-mile run.
Tuesday—3-mile run.
Wednesday—Weight training; 2-3-mile run.
Thursday 3-mile run.
Friday—Weight training; 2-3-mile run.
Saturday—5-mile run.
Sunday—Rest.

Spring
Monday—1x1000 (2:40); 2x800 (2:15); 2x600 (1:35), 4 minute rest between intervals; weight training; 4-mile run.
Tuesday—6 miles in 35 minutes.
Wednesday—1x800; 2x600; 2x400 (60 seconds); 4-mile run; weight training.
Thursday—1x600; 1x400; 2x200 (28 seconds); 5-mile run.
Friday—Stretch; warmup.

Saturday—Competition.
Sunday—Easy 3-mile run.

Summer
Monday—Weight training, 3-mile run.
Tuesday—3-mile fun run.
Wednesday—Weight training.
Thursday—4-mile fun run.
Friday—Weight training.
Saturday—Optional.
Sunday—Optional.

Pete Richardson

HERBERT "PETE" RICHARDSON   Berkeley High School

Born 4/19/63   Berkeley, California

6-2   154   Coach Willie White

COMPETITIVE BACKGROUND
Pete claims a National Prep Record in the 800 meters, California State and Golden West Invitational Championships and All-American honors as the highlights of his individual career. A member of one of the nation's finest high school track teams, he also has a piece of the national prep 4x400 relay record (3:08.94).

BEST TIMES
46.7(m,r)   1:47.31(m)

DAILY SEASONAL WORKOUTS
Fall
Monday—3x(8x220), jog 110 between each.
Tuesday—45-60-minute run.
Wednesday—1-hour fartlek run in hills.
Thursday—45-60-minute run.
Friday—3 x(10x110), jog 110 between each.
Saturday—1-hour run.
Sunday—1½-hour run.

Winter
Monday—2x330; 2x440; 2x550; 3x660.
Tuesday—1-hour run.

Wednesday—5x110; 5x165; 5x220; 5x330; 5x440.
Thursday—1-hour run.
Friday—5x330.
Saturday—1-hour run.
Sunday—1½-hour run.

Spring
Monday—660-550-440-330-220-110.
Tuesday—1-hour run.
Wednesday—45-minute fartlek run.
Thursday—6x220, with 220 jog between each.
Friday—30-minute run.
Saturday—Competition.
Sunday—1½-hour run.

Darrell Robinson
Calvin Kennon

DARRELL OTIS ROBINSON

Born 12/24/64

6-1½   140   Wilson High School

                        and   Tacoma, Washington

CALVIN EUGENE KENNON   Coach Jim Daulley

Born 1/3/63

6-0   152

COMPETITIVE BACKGROUND
The national's top one-lap pair from a single team, Robinson was tied for No. 10 on the 1981 list, while Kennon was No. 2 in the 400.

PREPARATION
The Wilson High School sprinters lift weights in the off-season:

Dead Lift	Incline Press	V-Ups
Cleans	Step-Ups	Dips
Bench Press	Sit-Ups	Leg work on Universal Machine

BEST TIMES
Robinson
10.4 20.88(m) 46.8(m) 1:57.4(m)

Kennon
10.4 21.2(m) 46.3(m) 1:55.8(m)

Calvin Kennon, Coach Daulley, Darrell Robinson

AGE GROUP MARKS

Year	Age		100		200	
	DR	CK	DR	CK	DR	CK
1977	12	13	11.0(y)	10.9(y)		24.4(y)
1978	13	14	10.4(y)	10.8(y)	22.9(y)	22.5(y)
1979	14	15	10.0(y)	9.9(y)	22.4(y)·	22.4(y)
1980	15	16	10.5(m)	10.5(m)	21.2(m)	21.5(m)
1981	16	17	10.4(m)	10.4(m)	20.9(m)	21.2(m)

Year	Age		400		800	
	DR	CK	DR	CK	DR	CK
1977	12	13		61.2(y)		
1978	13	14		50.8(y)		2:09.5(y)
1979	14	15	50.7(y)	48.7(m)		2:03.0(y)
1980	15	16	47.3(m)	47.5(m)		2:00.1(y)
1981	16	17	46.8(m)	46.3(m)	1:57.4(m)	1:55.8(m)

Calvin was serious about the strength work, while Darrell says he only "played around with the weights."

Warmups consisted of 15-20 minutes of stretching, an 800-1-mile jog, 5 minutes of stretching, and 3-4 forward and backward strides.

TRAINING COMMENTS

Both runners feel that early season work—step up 100s—were an excellent and important workout.

They psych-up with their team song, and feel it is important to go out hard in the long 400 sprint.

DAILY SEASONAL WORKOUTS

Fall

Run 8-10 miles each week.

Winter

Monday—Run 1-1½ miles to stadium, run a 15 minute circuit on the stairs, run back; or run 1½ miles to a 500-yard grass hill, run 3 hills; run back; light weight training.

Tuesday—3-mile golf course run.

Wednesday—1-mile warmup; stride 440 in 56 seconds; 1-mile warmdown; hard weight training.

Thursday—1-mile run on track in opposite direction; 1-mile run passing people and running to the front; 1-mile run on grass.

Friday—1-mile warmup; stride 1x660 with 440 in 60 seconds; 1-mile warmdown; hard weight training.

Saturday—1-mile jog.

Sunday—Rest.

Spring

Monday—1-mile jog, working on relay hand-offs; strides; run through relay 3-4 times at ½-speed; 1-mile warmdown.

Tuesday—½-mile warmup; *one* of the following:

    a) 550—through 440 in 53-54 seconds; 330 in 36 seconds;

    b) 660—through 440 in 58 seconds; 10 minute rest; 440 in 55 seconds;

    c) 3x330 in 38-37-36 seconds with a 5-minute rest between each;

    d) 5xparlaufs in 28 seconds;

    e) 330 in 37 seconds; 220 straight in 22.5 seconds; 330 in 37 seconds; 11-minute rest between each.

Weight training.

Wednesday—1-mile run on track in opposite direction; 1-mile run passing people and running to the front; 1-mile run in opposite direction.

Thursday—Same as Tuesday.

Friday—2-3-mile run; relay work.

Saturday—880 warmup; 1x660; 880 warmdown; weight training.

Sunday—Rest.

Summer

Monday—Hard 550—through 440 in 52 seconds; 330 in 35 seconds.

Tuesday—2-3-mile run.

Wednesday—Competition.

Thursday—2-3-mile run.

Friday—2-3-mile run.

Saturday—Competition.

Sunday—Rest.

David Timmons

DAVID GEFFERY TIMMONS   Oakland High School

Born 2/15/63   Oakland, California

6-0   138   Coaches Earl Lowe
                               David Ponas

COMPETITIVE BACKGROUND
David captured the 1981 California State Championship in the 400 meters in only his second year of track competition.

BEST TIMES
46.7(y)   1:56.4(y)

AGE GROUP MARKS

Year	Age	440
1980	17	49.7
1981	18	46.7, 45.8 (m,r)

PREPARATION
During the fall and winter David lifted weights twice each week:

Lateral Lifts	Lateral Pull Down
Curls	Bench Press

All lifts are done 2x8-10 repetitions with light weights.
He warmed up with an 880 jog, stretching, more jogging, easy 100s, and 8-10x100-yard accelerations.

TRAINING COMMENTS

Acceleration runs—10x100 with 30 yards of easy striding. Also, 30-yard pickups and a 40-yard sprint are an important part of every workout. Both David and Coach Ponas feel this is important as it put some speed into every workout. "In-and-Out" 330s—a combination of a fast 110, a 110 stride, and a fast, strong finishing 110—are also an important part of Dave's workout program. As the season progresses these are lengthened to 375-yard patterns. Overdistance work of 550-880 yards, high repetitions of 440s and pure speedwork make up the bulk of the remainder of Dave's practices.

DAILY SEASONAL WORKOUTS
Fall

Monday—3-mile run; 2x1320 (3:45), with a 440 walk between; 8x440 (68-70), with 220 walk between each.

Tuesday—3-mile run to X–C course; 6 sections of the course anywhere from 440 yards to 1 mile at 6:00 pace.

Wednesday—3-mile run; 1x880 (2:25); 6x330 (48); 4x220 (30).

Thursday—3-mile run; 2.4-mile X-C race; 1-2-mile run.

Friday—3-4-mile run; easy pace.

Saturday—3 miles of hill runs.

Sunday—Rest; or easy 2-3-mile run.

Winter

Monday—3-mile run (AM). 3-mile run; 1x880 (2:15) walk 440; 8-12x440 (64), walk 220 between each (PM).

Tuesday—3-mile run; 8x220 (27-28), jog 220 between each.

Wednesday—3-mile run (AM). 3-mile run at easy pace; 1x660 (1:35); 2x440 (62); 2x375 (50); 2x220 (26-27).

Thursday—3-mile run; 2x550 (75); 6-8x330 ins-and-outs (15-16-15).

Friday—3-mile run; baton work; 8x100 accelerations.

Saturday—Competition or easy 3-mile run.

Sunday—Rest.

Spring

Monday—3-mile run (AM). 3-mile run; 1x550 (71); 8x440 (under 60), with 6 minute rest between each (PM).

Tuesday—3-mile run; 6x375 (48); 4x220 (25).

Wednesday—Baton work; quick accelerations on grass; 4x220 (25).

Thursday—Dual meet—440-880-4x440 relay.

Friday—3-mile run; baton work; 6x100 strides; 2x220 (24-25).

Saturday—Relay meet.

Sunday—Rest.

Maxine Underwood

MAXINE UNDERWOOD	Brookline High School
Born 1/28/64	Brookline, Massachusetts
5-6 124	Coach Sherman Hart

COMPETITIVE BACKGROUND

The national Junior 400-meter champion began her track career as an eleven-year-old, when she filled in on her sister's track club relay team. Maxine also set a National H.S. indoor record of 34.5 for 300-yards.

BEST TIMES

10.8   11.9   24.4(y)   53.05(m)

AGE GROUP MARKS

Year	Age	100	220	440	880
1976	12	11.9	25.8	64.2	
1977	13	11.5	25.0	59.0	
1978	14	11.3	24.9	55.3	
1979	15	11.0		54.2(m)	2:14
1980	16	10.8(y)/11.8(m)	24.8y	53.74(m)	
1981	17	12.1(m)	24.4	53.05(m)	

PREPARATION

Maxine feels her fall cross-country work has been most important in building up her strength and endurance. She warms up before practice and competition with an 880 jog, 15-25 minutes of stretching, and six 100-yard progressions working from ¼-to ¾-speed.

TRAINING COMMENTS

Short   50-yard   sprints   are   Maxine's   least   favorite

workout, preferring instead long 660 yard intervals. She does
no special speed or strength work, gets psyched-up by her
coach's yelling, and simply likes to go out hard and fast in
the one lap sprint.

DAILY SEASONAL WORKOUTS
Fall
Monday—5 miles easy.
Tuesday—Speedwork: 220 runs on grass at ½ speed.
Wednesday—3 miles easy.
Thursday—Speedwork: uphill runs working on knee lift and arm action.
Friday—5 miles easy.
Saturday—Rest.
Sunday—Rest.

Winter
Monday—3x660 between 1:38-1:42; 4x80 at ½-speed.
Tuesday—7x220 between 28-31 seconds.
Wednesday—4x330 between 40-43 seconds; 4x100 at ½-speed.
Thursday—50-yard sprints from blocks at 9/10ths; relay work.
Friday—Rest.
Saturday—Competition.
Sunday—Rest.

All workouts begin with a ½-hour warmup and finish with a warmdown. Recovery time for intervals was to walk the distance run.

Spring
Monday—30-minute fartlek run.
Tuesday—7x220 between 30-35 seconds.
Wednesday—5x440 between 61-65 seconds.
Thursday—14x110 at 2/3-speed.
Friday—Rest.
Saturday—Competition.
Sunday—Rest.

Summer
Monday—3x660 between 1:38-1:42.
Tuesday—10x110 at 2/3-speed; block-work.
Wednesday—4x330 between 40-43 seconds.
Thursday—10x50 at 9/10ths speed; block-work.
Friday—Relay work.
Saturday—Competition.
Sunday—Rest.

SPRINTERS

Barbara Bell

BARBARA KAY BELL   Trimble Technical High School

Born 5/5/63   Fort Worth, Texas

5-5   125   Coach Tim Lewelling

COMPETITIVE BACKGROUND
Barbara began running in the fourth grade; by her senior year, she was a Texas high school All-Star and her team's most valuable athlete.

BEST TIMES
11.3(m)   23.6(m)

AGE GROUP MARKS

Year	Age	100m	200m
1978	15		26.0
1979	16		24.9
1980	17		23.9
1981	18	11.5	23.6

PREPARATION
Barbara works out two days each week on a Universal Gym Machine, two sets of ten repetitions at maximum weight on the Bench Press, Military Press, Lat Pulls, Curls, Leg Press, and Knee Machine. Before practice she warms up with static stretching and a 440 jog; before competition she adds 3 or 4 strides down the infield.

TRAINING COMMENTS

Although long intervals are her least favorite workout, if she could "do it over," Barbara says that she would do more practice work over 400 meters. Her favorite speed drill is a run on grass with an exaggerated pumping of the arms and high-knee lift.

DAILY SEASONAL WORKOUTS
Fall
Volleyball.

Winter
Monday—Weight training.
Tuesday—4-mile run.
Wednesday—Weight training.
Thursday—4-mile run.
Friday—2-mile run.
Saturday—Rest.
Sunday—Rest.

Spring
Monday—4x440; 4x220.
Tuesday—6x330; baton exchanges.
Wednesday—7x220, baton exchanges.
Thursday—4x165; 4x110, block-work; baton exchanges.
Friday—Stretch; or prelims for Saturday's meet.
Saturday—Competition.
Sunday—Rest.

Summer
Monday—2x330; 1x500; 5x110; baton exchanges; jog 440.
Tuesday—2x200; 1x330; 5x110; baton exchanges; jog 440.
Wednesday—1x550; 1x330; 1x220; 5x110 on grass; baton exchanges; jog 440.
Thursday—1x400; 5x110 on grass; baton exchanges; jog 440.
Friday—Rest.
Saturday—Competition.
Sunday—Rest.

Clyde Bishop

CLYDE E. BISHOP   Jack Yates High School

Born 5/29/62   Houston, Texas

6-0   177   Coach Bush

COMPETITIVE BACKGROUND
A member of the National Junior record-holding 4x100-meter relay team (40.4), Bishop was also Texas "Four Cities" sprint champion, and a national Junior medal winner in the 100-and 200-meter sprints. Clyde began competing at age 13.

BEST TIMES
9.3(y)   10.1(m)   21.0(m)

AGE GROUP MARKS

Year	Age	100	220/200
1978	15	9.6(y)	21.5(y)
1979	16	9.3(y)	21.0(m)
1980	17	9.4/10.3	20.5(r)
1981	18	10.1(m)	

PREPARATION
Clyde credits his winter weight-training program—an overall strength program 5 days each week—and overdistance work, as the most important parts of his training program. When the competitive season begins, he stops his upper-body weight-work, but continues the leg lifts until the championship season.

Bishop does not have any special flexibility drills, but employs thorough pre-practice and pre-competition warmup routines.

Pre-practice: 15-20 minutes stretching, 880 jog, 10 minutes stretching.

Pre-competition: 1-mile jog, 20 minutes stretching, 10-15x100 runs, stretching, block-work.

DAILY SEASONAL WORKOUTS
Fall Football.

Winter
Monday—Weight training:

Bench Press	5x1	165#
Leg Curl	3x3-5	15# each leg
Leg Curl	3x3-5	25# both legs
Arm Curl	5x3-5	50#

Tuesday—Weight training:

Bench Press	3x3-5	165#
Leg Curls	3x3-5	15# each leg
Leg Curls	3x3-5	25# both legs

2-mile run.
Wednesday—Same as Monday.
Thursday—Same as Tuesday.
Friday—Same as Monday.
Saturday—2-4-mile run; block-work.
Sunday—2-4 miles.

Spring
Monday—Weight training:

Leg Curls	9x3-5	15#

5x440; 6x220; 5x110 build-ups.
Tuesday—Weight training:

Leg Curls	9x3-5	15#

2x880; 5x110 build-ups; relay work.
Wednesday—Same as Monday.
Thursday—Same as Tuesday.
Friday—Same as Monday.
Saturday—2-4 miles.
Sunday—Rest.

Summer
Monday—Friday—3x440; 4x330; block-work.
Saturday—2-4 miles.
Sunday—Rest.

Darwin Cook

DARWIN RICHARD COOK   H.D. Woodson High School

Born 7/16/62   Washington, D.C.

5-10½   170   Coach Stan L. Mullings

COMPETITIVE BACKGROUND

Darwin first went out for track to stay in shape for soccer. Since then he has become city champion, All-Metro and high school All-American, the nation's top-ranked high school indoor sprinter, and the national prep recordholder in the 70-yard dash.

BEST TIMES

9.4 10.3 21.2(m) 21.4(y) 48.5(m)   6.23(60y AT)
5.9(55m) 6.8(70y)

AGE GROUP MARKS

Year	Age	60y	70y	100	200
1978	15			10.1(y)	
1979	16			9.7(y)	21.4(m)
1980	17			9.4(y)	
1981	18	6.23	6.8	10.3(m)	21.2(m)

PREPARATION

Darwin worked with weights 3 days each week during the winter season when, as a short sprinter, he had more time:

Monday—free weights	Wednesday—Universal Gym Machine
Clean & Press 2x5-7 85#	Leg Curls 2x5-7 85#

Curls	2x5-7 85#	Leg Kick	2x25-50
Bent-over Row	2x5-7 85#	Toe Raise	1x100
Bench Press	2x5-7 85#		

Friday:
1 set of Monday's workout;
1 set of Wednesday's workout;
2 sets on Leaper Machine.

TRAINING COMMENTS

"At Woodson High school, all of the sprinters use the 'recoil start.' I am right-handed and I kick with my right foot, so I would say that my right side is my power side. With this in mind, I try to get as much power and quickness out of the blocks as possible.

"I know my starting technique may go against some established principles, but I have had great success with it. My right foot is at the very front of the blocks—this gives me a 'recoil or cocked' sensation as if being shot from a cannon. My left foot is about 6½" from the back of the block. When I'm in the 'set' position, this leg is almost extended straight back so that it can be driven through quickly and smoothly on the gun. The recoil block placement is half bunch and half elongated.

"The secret to my start is the vigorous use of my arms out of the blocks. If done correctly, the explosive action of the recoil or cocked drive will spring you out, not up from the blocks. The arms are used to counter-balance the explosive action and to keep me on balance throughout the start. The basic starting techniques of weight well forward, neck relaxed, and mind alert also play a major role in getting a good start."

DAILY SEASONAL WORKOUTS
Fall
    Football.

Winter
    Monday—10x110 yards in 14 seconds; or 5 man continuous relays; weight training.
    Tuesday—6x200 in 30 seconds.

Wednesday—10x110 yards; continuous relays, weight training.
Thursday—Relay work; starts.
Friday—2x60 yards on time; 1x150 yards on time, 1x352 yards on time.
Saturday—Rest.
Sunday—Rest.
Winter workouts are done in the school hallways—200 yards around.

Spring

Monday—2x300 yards in 32-33 seconds.
Tuesday—5x220 step downs.
Wednesday—2x60 yards on time; 3x150 yards.
Thursday—6 gun starts; work on finish technique.
Friday—Easy run on football field or relay work.
Saturday—Competition.
Sunday—Rest.

Summer

Monday—Starts; 3x in-and-out 220s.
Tuesday—Rest.
Wednesday—Starts; from work on curve; 150s.
Thursday—Rest.
Friday—Technique work.
Saturday—Competition.
Sunday—Rest.

Marcus Currie

MARCUS CURRIE

Born 2/16/63

5-7½   160

Hillsboro High School

Nashville, Tennesse

Coach Chuck Lewis

COMPETITIVE BACKGROUND

Eventual State champion, All-American, and national recordholder in the sprints, Marcus discovered his speed when, as a youngster, he was able to beat his friends in running games. He began competing at age 14 in junior high school.

BEST TIMES

6.1(60y)   9.3   10.3   21.0(y)   49.5(y)

AGE GROUP MARKS

Year	Age	60y	100	220	440
1978	15		10.3(y)	22.5	
1979	16		9.7(y)	21.7	
1980	17		9.3(y)	21.0	49.5
1981	18	6.1	10.3(m)		

PREPARATION

Marcus works with weights—Bench Press, Clean & Press, and Squats; he also does a basic flexibility program, and warms up before practice and competition with a 1-mile run and 15 minutes of stretching.

TRAINING COMMENTS

Running hills and steps—a caring coach—were the most

important parts of Marcus's training program. If he could "do it over," he says that he would work harder.

DAILY SEASONAL WORKOUTS
Fall
Monday—4-5-mile run.
Tuesday—Rest.
Wednesday—Hill work.
Thursday—Rest.
Friday—4-5-mile run.
Saturday—Rest.
Sunday—Rest.

Winter
Monday—Weight training; 8x80 yards at medium speed.
Tuesday—5x20 yards with high knees; 5x20 yards skipping; 6x40 yard form runs.
Wednesday—Block-work; 10x20 yards; 6x60 yards.
Thursday—Weight training; 3-mile run.
Friday—Rest.
Saturday—Rest.
Sunday—Rest.

Spring
Monday—Weight training; 2x300; 2x150; 2x80; 1-mile cool-down.
Tuesday—Block-work; 4x20 yards; 15x60 yards; work on basic form.
Wednesday—Weight training; 10x130 yard runs on football field.
Thursday—Rest.
Friday—Competition.
Saturday—Competition.
Sunday—Rest.

Summer
Light form-work every day and compete in the Junior Olympics program.

Kelvin Freeman

KELVIN FREEMAN	Lake Taylor High School
Born 8/7/63	Norfolk, Virginia
5-5½ 153	Coach Floyd Conley

COMPETITIVE BACKGROUND
The son of a professional boxer, Kelvin started running by doing road work with his father.

BEST TIMES
6.2(55m)   9.3   10.1   21.5(m)   48.2(m)

AGE GROUP MARKS

Year	Age	100	200	400	600
1978	14				1:51
1979	15	9.8/10.5	21.9	51.0	1:32
1980	16	9.5	21.6	49.0	1:19
1981	17	9.3/10.2	21.3	48.2	

PREPARATION
Before practice, Kelvin warms up with a 3-lap jog and flexibility work, an 880 jog, and 10 pop-starts from the blocks get him ready for competition.

TRAINING COMMENTS
Kelvin feels that the training he likes least—440 workout—is the training which helps him the most. If he could "do it over again," he would change nothing, feeling that his workouts were as good as anyone's.

DAILY SEASONAL WORKOUTS
Fall
Monday—2-mile run after football practice.
Tuesday—4x300; block-work.
Wednesday—10x60-yard sprints; 1x300.
Thursday—Leg workout.
Friday—Football game.
Saturday—5x300; 10x60 yard sprints.
Sunday—3-mile run.

Winter
Monday—50 starts from blocks.
Tuesday—15 continuous runs, up and down a 40-yard hallway.
Wednesday—3x300; 10x60-yard sprints.
Thursday—5x500; starting block work.
Friday—3-mile run.
Saturday—3x300; 5x60 yard sprints.
Sunday—Leg exercises.

Spring
Monday—5 hill-sprints; 1x600-yard run.
Tuesday—10x100-yard sprints; 30 starts from blocks.
Wednesday—5x200; 10 starts from blocks.
Thursday—50 starts from blocks.
Friday—Light technique practice.
Saturday—3-mile run.
Sunday—Leg exercises.

Summer
Monday—6x300; 10x100-yard sprints.
Tuesday—2x200; 3x300; starting-block work.
Wednesday—3x200; 5x110; 4x100 strides on grass.
Thursday—2x300; 2x110; relay work.
Friday—Run bleachers; work on curve running.
Saturday—Competition.
Sunday—Rest.

Bruce Hardy
Clayton Beauford

BRUCE HARDY

Born 12/20/62   Palatka High School

5-9 140   Palatka, Florida

and   Coach Ken Brauman

CLAYTON BEAUFORD

6-0   175

COMPETITIVE BACKGROUND
This pair of super-sprinters first came out for track as 9th and 10th graders when Coach Braumen got them interested in the sport. Together they have garnered numerous Florida State championships, major invitational titles, and All-American honors.

BEST TIMES
Hardy
10.7   21.1(m)   46.88(m)

Beauford
10.6   21.5(m)   48.0(m)

AGE GROUP MARKS

Year	Age	100m BH	100m CB	200m BH	200m CB	400m BH	400m CB	300mIH BH
1978	15	11.9		24.2				
1979	16			23.2		49.8	50.3	38.5
1980	17		11.0	22.0	22.0	48.1	49.4	38.0
1981	18	10.7	10.6	21.1	21.5	46.88	48.0	

PREPARATION

The sprinters warm up with an 880 jog, stretching, 6x400 high-knee sprints, and additional sprinting. Bruce Hardy adds, "it is important that at some time in the warmup I run at top speed to prepare my muscles."

Both worked with weights three three days each week:

Bench Press   Power Cleans   Leg Curls
Curls   Squats   Heel Raises

All lifts were done 4 sets of 6-8 reps., increasing the weight from 70% to 100% of maximum.

TRAINING COMMENTS

Clayton feels that hill training has been the most important part of his training; Bruce stresses pre-season strength training and late-season speedwork. Both athletes feel that learning to relax at top speed had great importance. Form running at gradually-increasing speeds, concentrating on correct technique is used to work on this relaxation and prevent "breakdown" in the latter part of races.

They feel that super preparation psyched them up for races—they knew they "were ready to race whenever they stepped on the track." Both prefer to go out hard in the 400, with an especially-hard sprint through the third 110. In the 200, they feel that running a hard turn and maintaining technique down the stretch is the key.

DAILY SEASONAL WORKOUTS
Fall

Monday—2-3-mile run.
Tuesday—Hill work—10 sprints up and down.
Wednesday—2-3-mile run.
Thursday—660-440-330-220-110.
Friday—2-3-mile run.
Saturday—Athlete's choice of workout or rest.
Sunday—Rest.
Weight Training on Monday, Wednesday, and Friday.

Winter

Monday—Hill work—15-20 sprints up and down.
Tuesday—660-440-330-220-110.
Wednesday—15-20x220 under 30 seconds.

Thursday—5-10x165 sprints 110 jog-55 sprint.
Friday—Hill work—15-20 sprints up and down.
Saturday—Overdistance work.
Sunday—Rest.
Weight Training on Monday, Wednesday, and Friday.

Spring

Monday—4x280 at full-speed, 5-10-minute recovery.
Tuesday—6-8x220 strides at ¾-speed on grass.
Wednesday—Hill work—8-10 sprints up and down.
Thursday—5x165 sprint-110 jog-55 sprint.
Friday—Relay work; technique work.
Saturday—Competition.
Sunday—Rest.
Weight Training on Monday, Wednesday, and Friday.

Summer

Summer training consists of weight training, technique work, and a combination of workouts of choice depending upon the level at which the athlete is still competing.

Treye Jackson

TREYE JACKSON   Newton High School

Born 11/2/61   Newton, Iowa

6-1   180   Coach Lenny Dunman

COMPETITIVE BACKGROUND

Treye, Iowa State Champion in the sprints, started competing in track at age eight when he was introduced to the sport by his father.

BEST TIMES

10.3   21.2(m)   47.5(m)

PREPARATION

Treye works with weights during the winter and spring seasons.

Leg Lifts	10x6
Curls	8x6
Leaper Machine	5x35
Sit-Ups	100 before and 50 after practice.

He warms up with jogging and stretching before practice and meets. Treye eats light, avoids junk food, and takes vitamins to hold his weight steady and keep up his strength during the season.

TRAINING COMMENTS

"There is no real strategy for the sprints except get out of the blocks fast and stay out in front." Treye does feel that strong arm-drive is important in the 200 meters to be strong through the corner.

DAILY SEASONAL WORKOUTS
Fall
Football.

Winter
Monday—Flexibility exercises and run stairs.
Tuesday—Weight training.
Wednesday—Jog 2 miles.
Thursday—Weight training.
Friday—10x20 yard sprints; run stairs.
Saturday—Weight training.
Sunday—Jog 4 miles.

Spring
Monday—Flexibility.
Tuesday—Flexibility and sprint work.
Wednesday—3x550; 2x440; 3x330; 2x220; 5x110; 2x50.
Thursday—Weight training and jog 2 miles.
Friday—Competition.
Saturday—Competition or jog 1 mile and 3x440.
Sunday—Jog 4 miles.

Summer
Continue spring workouts until the start of summer football practice.

La Shon Nedd

LA SHON ANNETTE NEDD	Skyline High School
Born 6/8/63	Dallas, Texas
5-6 125	Coach Mary Ann Thomas

COMPETITIVE BACKGROUND
La Shon's track participation began in elementary school, through competing in Jesse Owens track meets. She concluded her high school career as the nation's fastest ranking half-lap sprinter.

BEST TIMES
11.24(m)   22.8w(m)   54.06(m)

AGE GROUP MARKS
Year	Age	100m	200m	400m
1976	12		25.6	
1978	14		26.3	
1979	15		24.6	
1980	16		26.1	
1981	17	11.64	23.0	54.06

PREPARATION
La Shon warms up with stretching, a 1-2-lap jog, more stretching and 2x40-yard runs with giant strides. Her summer track club adds more jogging and 6x100 yard runs to the warmup.

During the cross country season she works out on a Hydra-gym Machine with 20-second sessions for hamstrings, quads, arms and legs.

TRAINING COMMENTS
"Learning to relax in the short sprints by running the 400 meters" is the most important part of LaShon's training.

DAILY SEASONAL WORKOUTS
Fall and Winter
Monday—2-mile run.
Tuesday—2-mile run; weight training.
Wednesday—2-mile run.
Thursday—2-mile run; weight training.
Friday—1-mile run.
Saturday—Cross country meet.
Sunday—1-mile run.

Spring
The same workout is done twice each day, 11:30 AM and 4:00PM.
Monday—4x100; baton exchanges.
Tuesday—2-3x330.
Wednesday—2-3x220; baton exchanges.
Thursday—4x100; baton exchanges; no PM workout.
Friday—Competition—prelim's.
Saturday—Competition—finals.
Sunday—1-mile jog.

Summer
Monday—2x100 bounding; 2x100 with high knees, 2x100.
Tuesday—200, rest 2 minutes; 100, walk back; 200, rest; 100, walk back; 200.
Wednesday—2x300.
Thursday—Block-work; 40-60-80-120, and back down the ladder.
Friday—1-mile jog.
Saturday—Competition.
Sunday—1-mile jog.

Van Pearcy

VAN MARK PEARCY

Andrews High School

Born 10/3/62

Andrews, Texas

6-2   178

Coach Bob Isbell

COMPETITIVE BACKGROUND

All-American honors in track and football, three years of runner-up honors at the Texas State meet, International Prep and Golden West second-place finishes, and a national Juniors medal have highlighted Van's outstanding high school athletic career.

BEST TIMES

10.41   21.12(m)   46.8(m)   46.0(r)

AGE GROUP MARKS

Year	Age	100	220/200	400
1975	12	11.6(y)		
1976	13	10.7(y)		
1977	14	10.4(y)	22.9(y)	
1978	15	9.9(y)	22.2(y)	
1979	16		21.4(m)	47.3(m)
1980	17	9.6(y)	21.2(m)	46.8(m)
1981	18	10.41(m)	21.3(m)	47.1(m)
				hamstring injury

PREPARATION

Van lifted weights twice each week during his senior year.

Bench Press	3x10	185#	Hamstring Lift	2x10	
Cleans	3x10	160#	Chin-Ups	3x15	

| Squats | 2x7 | 240# | Bench Jumps | 3x15 seconds |
| Lat Pulls | 3x10 | 175# | | with 25# vest |

To warm up for practice and meets, Van jogs 2-4 laps, stretches, runs 10x100 build ups, runs two all-out 100s; then he is really ready to run.

TRAINING COMMENTS

Being able to run against quality runners has been an important part of Van's track progress. His favorite workout is 8x200 in 23-24 seconds, but if he could "do it over again" he would run faster in practice and try not to get injured.

For a race pattern in the 400, "I go out and run the first 100 pretty hard, then I keep the pace, running relaxed but fast; the 200 will usually be from 21.4-22.2. I keep the pace—if possible—all the way by concentrating on relaxing and running fast."

DAILY SEASONAL WORKOUTS
Fall
Football.

Winter
Football and run mileage.

Spring
Monday—Weight training; 2-mile warmup; 1x500 at ¼-½-speed; 3x200 in 27 seconds; warmdown.
Tuesday—1-mile warmup; 8x200 in 27 seconds; warmdown.
Wednesday—Weight training; 2-mile warmup; 3x300; 2-mile warmdown.
Thursday—1-mile warmup; warmdown.
Friday—Dual meet.
Saturday—Rest.
Sunday—2-mile run.

Summer
Monday—Weight training; 880 jog; warmup; 2x500; 2x200 in 25 seconds; warmdown.
Tuesday—800 jog, warmup 6-8x220 in 24-25 seconds; warmdown.
Wednesday—Weight training; warmup; 4x300 in 37 seconds; warmdown.
Thursday—880 jog, warmup, 4x150 at 400 pace; starting block work; warmdown.
Friday—Warmup; warmdown.
Saturday—Competition—400-200-4x400 relay-LJ-HJ.
Sunday—2-mile jog.

Ken Robinson
Sharon Ware

KENNETH ROBINSON

Born 7/15/63

5-9   140   Berkeley High School

and   Berkeley Eastbay Track Club

SHARON WARE   Coaches Willie White, Arno Brewer

Born 9/27/63

5-0   106

COMPETITIVE BACKGROUND

A pair of two-time *Scholastic Coach* All-Americans, both Ken and Sharon have TAC Junior and California State Championships to their credit. Ken's interest in track began when he entered high school, while Sharon joined the Eastbay Track Club as an 11-year-old.

BEST TIMES
Robinson
5.89(50m)   6.34(60y)   10.39(m)   21.03(m) 46.8(m)
Ware
6.42(50m)   11.34(m)   23.62(m)   39.6(300m)

AGE GROUP MARKS

Year	Age	50m/60y	100		200		400
		KR	KR	SW	KR	SW	KR
1978	14		10.34(y)	10.7(y)	24.4(y)	23.9(w,y)	
1979	15		9.9(y)	11.79(m)	23.0(y)	24.15(m)	51.2(y)
1980	16	5.89(m)	10.59(m)	11.34(m)	21.21(m)	23.62(m)	47.0(r)
1981	17	6.34(y)	10.39(m)	11.59(m)	21.03(m)	24.04(m)	46.3(r)

PREPARATION

Both Kenny and Sharon work with weights during the season. Sharon states that this work was sometimes inconsistent because other Phys-Ed classes had priority in the weight room.

Weight Training Program

Universal Gym		Free Weights	
Bench Press	Abdominal Curls	Sit Ups	Dead Lift
Overhead Press	Leg Press	Bench Press	¼-Squats
Rowing	Toe Press	Overhead Press	Calf Raises
Fore-Arm Curls	Leg Extension	Rowing	
Dead Lift	Hamstring Curls		

Fall—3x8 repetitions at 66.7% of maximum with a 3-minute rest between sets.

Winter and Spring—3x4 repetitions at 80-90% of maximum, with a 5-minute rest between sets.

The Berkeley stars use a complete and complex warmup program:

Pre-Practice	*Pre-Competition*
1) 10-15 minute run (fall-winter); or 1-mile jog (spring-summer);	1) 1-mile jog;
2) 3-5x50 easy;	2) 3-6x50m medium;
3) upper-body flexibility drills;	3) upper and lower body flexibility drills;
4) 3-5x50m medium;	4) 8-12x100m accelerations;
5) lower body flexibility drills;	5) sprint drills;
6) 3-5x50m medium (fall-winter); or 8-14x100m accelerations (spring-summer).	6) 6-8x50m fast;
	7) report in during 2nd call and stay loose.

TRAINING COMMENTS

Ken feels that the fall and winter portions of his training program have been the most important; Sharon agrees and adds that the endurance and hill work and the technique-work sprint-drills formed a strong base for their long competitive season. A positive attitude and competitive toughness combine with aggressive race tactics to keep the sprinters relaxed and in total control of their running form throughout their races.

Berkeley sprint drills use combinations of high knee or leg extension skipping, long skipping, and running. Drills are done in sets of 3-5 repetitions of 20-30 meters.

DAILY SEASONAL WORKOUTS

Fall

Monday—Warmup; sprint drills; 2-4x (10x150); or 2-4x (10x100); strength-endurance drills; weight training.

Tuesday—Warmup; medicine ball drills; jump drills; 6x300m.

Wednesday—30-minute fartlek run, warmup; sprint drills; strength-endurance drills; weight training.

Thursday—Warmup; medicine-ball drills; jump drills; 2x100; 3x150; 4x100; 3x150; 2x150.

Friday—Warmup, sprint drills; 100-200-200; 300-200-200;

200-200-100; or 200-meter build-ups.
Saturday—Rest.
Sunday—Rest.

Winter

Monday—Warmup; sprint drills; 4-5x250-500; weight training.
Tuesday—Warmup; power/speed drills; 6x330-yard hills.
Wednesday—Warmup; sprint drills; jump drills; strength endurance drills; weight training.
Thursday—Warmup; power speed drills; 6-8x150-200-meter hills; or 4x200, 3x200, 2x200.
Friday—Warmup; sprint drills; 6x100-250; weight training.
Saturday—Competition or rest.
Sunday—Rest.

Early Spring

Monday—Warmup; sprint drills, 3-4x200-500.
Tuesday—Warmup; 3-4x100-meter accelerations; 5x30m (medium); 5x30m (fast); 4x60m (fast); 2-4x30m (fast with flying start).
Wednesday—Warmup; sprint drills; 6x150-250.
Thursday—Dual meet; or warmup; 3-5x100-200 accelerations; 5x30m (medium); 5x30m (fast); 5x60m (fast); 5x60m (fast).
Friday—Warmup; relay practice; or Thursday's practice, if dual meet was Thursday.
Saturday—Competition.
Sunday—Rest.

Late Spring

Day 1—Warmup; sprint drills; 2-3x150-300.
Day 2—Warmup; 4-8x60-100 relay passes; 1x300 (fast).
Day 3—Warmup; 10-12x100 on grass; starts with 30-40-meter sprint.
Day 4—Warmup; 4-6x80-100 relay passes.
Day 5—Warmup; sprint drills; 1-2x (8x100).
Late spring practice is run on a 5-day rotation which varies with the meet schedule; rest days are assigned by the coach.
All school-day practices are from 7:30-9:30 AM.

Summer

    Day 1—Rest.
    Day 2—Warmup; sprint drills; 2-3x150.
    Day 3—Rest.
    Day 4—Rest.
    Day 5—Warmup; 6x70 meters with flying start; or 6x70 relay passes.
    Day 6—Warmup.
    Day 7—Warmup; 8x100.
    Day 8—Rest.
    Day 9—Warmup, 2x50m; 3x70m; 2x100m.
    Day 10—Rest.
    Day 11—Warmup; 4-5x30-meter gun starts.
    Day 12—Competition.
Summer practices are run on a 12-day rotation based on competition days.

Wallace Spearmon

WALLACE NATHANIAL SPEARMON

Born 9/3/62

6-2   170

Dwight D. Eisenhower
High School
Blue Island, Illinois

Coach Frank Gramarosso

COMPETITIVE BACKGROUND

Wallace began competing as a 10-year-old. A consistent place winner in Illinois State meets, he has won numerous local and regional awards, and is a national Junior Olympic medalist in both short sprints.

BEST TIMES

9.73   10.0(wind)   21.3(y)   20.7(m)

AGE GROUP MARKS

Year	Age	50	60	100	200	400
1973	10	6.5				
1974	11	6.3				
1975	12	6.2				
1976	13			11.5(y)		
1977	14			11.0(y)		
1978	15			10.2(y)	22.9(y)	
1979	16		6.5	9.73(y)	21.3(y)	
1980	17		6.25	10.5(m)	20.8(m)	
1981	18		6.20	10.44(mw)	20.89(m)	50.0

PREPARATION

Wallace does light upper-body and arm-lifting

throughout the year to maintain strength. His pre-practice warmup includes a 1-mile jog, hamstring, calf, and hip-flexibility work, partner stretches, sprint drills and striding. Twenty to thirty minutes before racing he jogs 2 laps, stretches and takes stride runs.

TRAINING COMMENTS

Spearman's coaches have handled the sprint star well. High school coach Gramarosso works hard to prevent over-work situations; whenever he is faced with a three-meet week, the competition days become the workout days and the off-days are used for technique work and active rest. Track club coach Donna Schulenburg solves the "no one fast enough to work out with" problem by handicapping Wallace with longer yardage against slower runners.

DAILY SEASONAL WORKOUTS
Fall

Monday—1-mile warmup; flex-stretch; 4x100 accelerations; cooldown jog.

Tuesday—1-mile warmup, flexibility, 1 mile easy, 2x100 strides, cooldown jog.

Wednesday—1 mile, strides, run over the first 2-3 hurdles of the 330 lows.

Thursday—2-3-mile run.
Friday—1-mile warmup; flexibility; sprint drills; strides.
Saturday—2-mile run or rest.
Sunday—Rest.

Winter

Monday—1-mile warmup; flexibility; strides; sprint drills; 10x100 build-ups; 1x600 with 1st 200 easy, 2nd moderate, 3rd strong; 800 cooldown.
Tuesday—1-mile warmup; flexibility; strides; sprint drills; 5x1 minute runs with 45-60-second rest between; starts.
Wednesday—1-mile warmup; flexibility; sprint drills; 10x100 build-ups; 4x300 in 38-42, walk 100 between; 5x150 build-ups; 800 jog.
Thursday—Same as Tuesday; relay work.
Friday—Easy warmup; starts.
Saturday—Competition.
Sunday—Rest.

Spring

Monday—Warmup; long intervals; starts; baton exchanges.
Tuesday—Dual meet; or hard sprint workout—4-6x100-400 intervals.
Wednesday—Starts; relay work.
Thursday—Dual meet; or hard sprint workout.
Friday—Starts; baton work.
Saturday—Invitational competition.
Sunday—Rest.

Summer

Monday—Warmup; 3x345(38-45); 3x160(16-18).
Tuesday—Warmup; 4x160(15-16); 4x120(11-12); 4x60(6-7); starts on turn and straight.
Wednesday—Warmup; 1x470(60-63); 1x350(42-45); 1x235(26-28); 2x160(16-17) 2x120(12-13).
Thursday—Warmup; 2x235(26-27); 3x160(16-17); 4x120(11-12).
Friday—Warmup; 10 straightaways, walking turn between each; starts on turn and straights.
Saturday—Competition.
Sunday—Rest.

AURORA RELAYS

SPRINTERS/HURDLERS

Piper Bressant

PIPER BESS BRESSANT   Jefferson-Huguenot-Wythe HS

Born 7/8/63   Richmond, Virginia

5-3½   111   Coach James Holdren

COMPETITIVE BACKGROUND
Now holder of 19 of her school's indoor and outdoor track and field records and a two-time All-American, Piper first joined the track team with her friends as a freshman.

BEST TIMES
13.76(100m 30"H)	14.16(100m 33"H)
60.61(400m H)	55.57(400m)

AGE GROUP MARKS

Year	Age	100m H	400m H	400m
1978	14	14.2	62.08	59.2(r)
1979	15	14.2 14.2	61.3	58.9
1980	16	13.8 14.3	61.4	57.9 injured
1981	17	13.5 13.9	60.61(AT)	55.57(AT)
		13.76(AT) 14.16(AT)		

PREPARATION
Piper used an extensive weight training program, lifting three days each week throughout the year.

Military Press	Leg Press
Bench Press	Knee Extensions
Arm Curls	Hamstring Curls
Upright Row	Sit-Ups

All lifts are done 5 sets of 5 reps each, except for sit-ups which are 1 set in 30 seconds.

The first set is done at 40% of maximum and each set is then increased by 5%. Each lifting session increases set #1 percentage by 5% until lifting is at 100%; then the athlete is retested for maximums. Arm and leg exercises are alternated during the lifting session and, on non-lifting days, athletes do one set of 50 reps on a Leaper Machine or one set of 50 bouncing split-squats.

TRAINING COMMENTS

Piper feels that the progressive building of endurance, strength, and speed through cross country, weight training, and then speedwork, respectively, has been the most important part of her training.

Her special "speed drill for short hurdlers" sets hurdles #1, 3, and 5, with #3 placed 4 feet closer to the start and #5 placed 8 feet closer. Seven steps are taken between the hurdles. She has also used speed-assisted towing, with ½" surgical tubing, as a speed drill. The athlete is towed by ½" surgical tubing approximately 10 yards long, which is stretched to 60-70 yards. The speed gains are up to .8 seconds in 30 meters over unassisted sprints.

DAILY SEASONAL WORKOUTS
Early Fall
　　Monday—3-6-mile run.
　　Tuesday—3-6-mile fartlek run.
　　Wednesday—3-6-mile hilly run.
　　Thursday—3-6-mile fartlek run.
　　Friday—3½-mile run; 2-3x1-mile loop with 10 exercise stations; 3½-mile run.
　　Saturday—5-8-mile run.
　　Sunday—Easy jog.

Late Fall
　　Monday—10-15x440 at faster than race pace.
　　Tuesday—3-5-mile easy run.
　　Wednesday—Dual meet.
　　Thursday—3-6-mile fartlek run.

Friday—Pace and hill work; or easy 3-5-mile run.
Saturday—6-10-mile run or competition.
Sunday—Easy jog.
Weight training done on Monday, Wednesday, and Friday throughout the season.

Early Winter
Monday—6x300 meters (58 seconds), with a 100 jog between each.
Tuesday—Hurdle drills and long jump pop-ups.
Wednesday—600-500-400-300-200 with a jog of equal distance between.
Thursday—15x100m; or 10x150m fast but relaxed.
Friday—Relay work.
Saturday—Rest; or minor competition.
Sunday—Rest; or jog.

Late Winter
Monday—Hurdle work.
Tuesday—6x300m (47 seconds) with 100m jog between each.
Wednesday—300-255-220-185-150 with a 5-minute rest between each—distances were run at set goal-times.
Thursday—15x100 or 10x150; long jump work.
Friday—Relay work; or rest.
Saturday—Competition.
Sunday—Rest; or jog.
Weight training done on Monday, Wednesday, and Friday throughout the season (day off before big meets). On Tuesday and Thursday, steps (50° and 35-feet long) are run with 2.5 pounds in each hand, starting with 1 set of 5 and increasing over the weeks to 2 sets of 10.

Early Spring
Monday—Hurdle work; speed-assisted sprint work.
Tuesday—200-400-600-500-300-100—jog equal distance between.
Wednesday—225-220-185-150-115 at goal times with a 5-minute rest between each, distances and times decrease as the season progresses.
Thursday—10x150 or 15x100.

Friday—Relay work.
Saturday—Easy jog; or minor competition.
Sunday—Rest; or jog.

Late Spring
Monday—Hurdle work.
Tuesday—10x150; or 15x100, fast but relaxed.
Wednesday—Dual meet.
Thursday—10x150; or 15x100, fast but relaxed.
Friday—Rest.
Saturday—Competition.
Sunday—Rest; or jog.

Weight training on Monday, Wednesday, and Friday throughout the season (off before major competition). Step runs on Tuesday and Thursday.

Early Summer
Monday—500-300-200 fast with a 5-minute rest between each; or 5x200 over low hurdles.
Tuesday—3 sets of 5x100 (¼-½-¾-½-¼-effort), jogging 100 between each and walking 400 between sets; run-hop on 2 legs—hop on right leg—hop on left leg—repeat 5 times for 2 sets of 100 meters.
Wednesday—Hurdle work, 5xspeed drill; 5x30 meter speed-assisted sprintwork.
Thursday—Long jump steps; hurdle work; 2 sets of 5x100 meters.
Friday—Jog and stretch.
Saturday—Competition.
Sunday—Rest or jog.

Weight training done on Monday and Wednesday throughout the season, step runs done on Tuesdays.

Late Summer
Easy mileage work.

Debbie
Da Costa

DEBORAH ANN DACOSTA   Palmetto High School

Born 1/24/64   Miami, Florida

5-10½   140   Coach Dr. Bob Miller

COMPETITIVE BACKGROUND
Dr. Miller, the Sunshine Striders Track Club and high school coach, asked Debbie to go out for track after elementary school and junior high physical education teachers had informed him of her talent. *Miami News* "Track Athlete Of The Year," she is Florida State pentathlon champion and holds State records in the pentathlon and 110-yard hurdles.

BEST TIMES
13.5   24.7   42.50(330LH)   3684(pent)

AGE GROUP MARKS

Year	Age	220	110LH	330LH	Pent.
1979	14	injured			
1980	15	25.5	14.1	43.8	3495
1981	16	24.7	13.5	42.50	3685

PREPARATION
Fond of Jamaican cooking, Debbie says that "weight is a constant problem." To combat it, Coach Miller has her cut back on soda, candy, fried foods, and after-8p.m. eating to eliminate junk food.

Debbie works with weights 2-3 times each week:

¾-Squats	3x10	240#
Bent Rowing	3x10	100#
Leg Press	3x20	300#
Incline Press	3x10	80#
Overhead Curls	3x10	45#
Step-Ups	3x20	50#
Toe Raises	3x20	100#

For flexibility, Debbie uses both static and progressive stretching exercises. She warms up wearing knitted leg warmers until the last minute, before which she stretches, does hurdle trail-leg drills, starts, and some jogging. Her special flexibility drill is to hold the hurdle in both hands with one foot on top of the bar at 42", hopping in until the knee is against the chest, then hopping out.

TRAINING COMMENTS

If she could "do it over again," Debbie would have begun her weight training and off-season conditioning earlier in her career.

Debbie psychs-up for competition through prayer, thorough stretching, and mentally visualizing the entire race from the start, through each hurdle, to the finish. She likes to get her worrying over with the night before the competition.

"The 110 hurdles are too short for tactics. I think only of a quick snap of the trail leg and sprinting between the hurdles, not about hurdling itself. In the 330 hurdles, I concentrate on pressing as hard as possible through the first 220, then concentrating on maintaining top form as I tire slightly. As a right-leg leader, I like the fast competition on that side."

Debbie stresses that her workouts vary greatly from day to day, but that her training program is based on a hard-easy pattern. Many of the sprint and distance runs use tag games or cross country pursuit drills to add variety to practice. Debbie's workout program is individually designed for her, and only the teams "Year 'round runners" participate in such a strenuous program.

DAILY SEASONAL WORKOUTS
Fall

Monday—Weight training (AM). 3-4-mile run; flexibility drills (PM).

117

Tuesday—2-mile fartlek run; bounding; depth jumping.
Wednesday—3-4-mile run; flexibility drills.
Thursday—Weight training (AM). Bounding; depth jumping; rope jumping; stairs (PM).
Friday—1-mile jog; 15-30 minutes of hurdle work; grass sprinting.
Saturday—Swimming; light jogging.
Sunday—Stretch.
Debbie also plays on the volleyball team during the fall.

Winter
Monday—Weight training (AM). Distance run (PM).
Tuesday—Sprints; 3x(100-200-300-400-300-200-100).
Wednesday—2-mile-fartlek run; strength drills.
Thursday—Weight training (AM). 4-6x330 (45-48); jog 1-2 miles.
Friday—Starts and hurdles; grass sprints.
Saturday—Swimming; active rest.
Sunday—3-5-mile run; or interval work.

Spring
Monday—Meet preparation; relay drills; starts; form running.
Tuesday—Competition—generally 110 hurdles, 330 hurdles, and two other events.
Wednesday—Overdistance work at 440-660 yards—80-90%.
Thursday—Forty minutes of hurdle work; forty minutes of field event work; jog.
Friday—Sprint work.
Saturday—Active rest; other sports; hurdle at home for forty minutes.
Sunday—Varied-speed distance run.

Summer
Monday—Sprints; fartlek run; 220s; 330s; curves.
Tuesday—Hurdle work; field-event work.
Wednesday—6x50 from blocks; 4 laps sprinting curves; 4x "infield Xs".
Thursday—Hurdle work.
Friday—Pre-competition warmups; polishing.
Saturday—Competition.
Sunday—Rest.

Reggie Davis

REGINALD DAVIS

Born 1/17/64

6-2½   179

Lincoln High School

Tallahassee, Florida

Coach Pat Murphy

COMPETITIVE BACKGROUND

Reggie went out for track because he wanted to travel on trips with the team. This led to his becoming Florida State champion in the high and intermediate hurdles.

BEST TIMES
        13.8   38.4

AGE GROUP MARKS

Year	Age	120HH	330IH
1979	15	15.0	42.5
1980	16	14.5	40.0
1981	17	13.8	38.4

PREPARATION

Reggie works with weights during the winter season; 3x10 reps. at 80% of maximum for upper-body strength and performs hamstring exercises to help prevent injuries. He feels this weight-work and over-distance training have been very important, especially in providing the string base needed when training is cut back during the competitive season.

TRAINING COMMENTS

"When learning the hurdles I was made to approach each hurdle 'high stepping' with my knees very high. This taught me to 'step' the hurdle rather than jump.

"I concentrate on leading with my knee, not my feet. My lead knee must start first; I bring my knee up, then extend my foot, clearing the hurdle with my knee slightly bent. My trail-leg knee must be brought up high, then through. I try to imagine knocking an apple off the hurdle with my trail leg knee. Bringing the trail leg through is the key to being able to sprint between hurdles.

"Staying square over the hurdle is important. I do this by lining up on a hurdle. My head goes over the middle of the hurdle; my lead arm shoots down on the left side of the hurdle (this helps my lean); finally my lead leg goes over the right side of the hurdle, not the middle. I don't loop my leg, but bring it up at a 45° angle and down the same. When I clear the hurdle, I land square and on balance.

"I start my hurdle move by driving, pointing my head squarely at the middle of the hurdle. If I don't concentrate on this I find myself getting high, which causes me to lose momentum after I clear the hurdle.

"I try to concentrate on continuing my lean through the hurdle. This brings my lead-leg down. Many people make the mistake of trying to snap the leg down. This is wrong because many times it forces your body to stand up, thus bringing your trail leg down, either hitting the hurdle or cutting down the length of your follow-through. The lead leg will drop fast if you just continue to lean through the hurdle. I work a great deal on my trail leg. It is the most important part of hurdling. If the trail leg is bad, even sprinters cannot gain speed between the hurdles. If the trail leg is brought through, taking a big step, even a slow hurdler can sprint between the hurdles.

"Each day I do hurdle work I try to review the basics. Usually when I have a bad race, it is because I messed up some basic point in hurdle form. I always go back after a race and practice the basic points that I feel cost me time."

DAILY SEASONAL WORKOUTS
Fall

Football.

120

Winter

Monday—Weight training; 3-5 miles LSD; or hills.
Tuesday—2 sets of 5x330 (45-50 seconds); or 4x440 (65-70 seconds).
Wednesday—Weight training, 5 miles LSD; or hills.
Thursday—Strength; hurdle work; 2x660 in 1:40.
Friday—Weight training; 2 miles in 12 minutes.
Saturday—Rest.
Sunday—Rest.

Spring

Monday—3-mile trail run; hurdle work; 6x330 (40-42 seconds).
Tuesday—Competition.
Wednesday—5-mile trail run; stretch over hurdles; 5 step hurdles; work on yesterday's mistakes.
Thursday—110-220-330-440-660 at 60 second quarter pace, no hurdles.
Friday—Stretch; 20 starts over 3 hurdles; 3-mile trail run.
Saturday—Competition.
Sunday—Rest.

Summer

"I do a lot of bike riding, 10-20 miles a day or more, compete on Thursdays, and do hurdle work two days a week."

Eric Jones

J. ERIC JONES   Beatrice Senior High School

Born 7/18/62   Beatrice, Nebraska

6-2   180   Coaches Willis Jones
                                                              Neil Henry

COMPETITIVE BACKGROUND

Son of the high school track coach, J. Eric started competing at age 7 in local AAU meets. Nebraska State champion in the 300-meter intermediate hurdles, he has twice placed 6th at the national Junior Olympics.

BEST TIMES

14.2   37.46(m)   53.71(m)

AGE GROUP MARKS

Year	Age	100	400	60y HH	110m HH	300m HH	400m IH
1972	9	12.6					
1974	11	11.8					
1976	13		56.1				
1978	15			7.8			
1979	16				15.2		
1980	17				14.6		
1981	18					37.46	53.71

PREPARATION

J. Eric warms up with a jog, stretching, and 150 yard runs until he works up a good sweat.

TRAINING COMMENTS

If he could "do it over again," Jones says he would add weight training to his workouts. His favorite workouts are 400-and 300-meter runs; he feels that this running and "putting in the time" has been the most important part of his training.

In the intermediate hurdles, Eric takes 22 steps to the first hurdle and 15 steps between hurdles. To psych-up for races, he convinces himself that he is going to win, concentrates hard on being smooth over the hurdles, and goes all-out, feeling it is important to go out fast.

DAILY SEASONAL WORKOUTS
Fall
> Basketball.

Winter
> Basketball.

Spring
> Monday—6x3HH; 12-15x150.
> Tuesday—3x3IH; 10x330.
> Wednesday—6x3HH; 12x200.
> Thursday 8x150.
> Friday—Stretch.
> Saturday—Competition.
> Sunday—5x300.

Summer
> Monday—3x3IH; 10x300.
> Tuesday—5x3HH; 8x400.
> Wednesday—3x3IH; 12x150.
> Thursday—5x3HH; 10x200.
> Friday—3x3IH; 5x150; 3x200.
> Saturday—8x300.
> Sunday—4x150; 4x300.

Norman Stafford, Jr.

NORMAN MARCUS STAFFORD, JR.   Angleton High School

Born 2/28/64   Angleton, Texas

5-8   155   Coach James Leonard

COMPETITIVE BACKGROUND
A National Junior Olympic medalist and national age-group recordholder in the 400 intermediate hurdles, Norman first went out for track to join his junior high friends.

BEST TIMES
47.4(r)   38.2(300IH)   53.1(400IH)

AGE GROUP MARKS

Year	Age	440	300IH	400IH
1978	14	54.2(r)		
1979	15	52.6(r)	40.8	
1980	16	47.4(r)	38.2	53.1

PREPARATION
Norman worked with weights 3 days each week during the winter and twice a week during early spring.

Toe Raises	3x12	Bench Press	3x8
Rowing	3x8	Leg Curls	3x12
Squats	3x12	Military Press	3x8
Lat Pulls	3x8	Sit-Ups	3x12
Leg Press	3x12	Arm Curls	3x8

TRAINING COMMENTS

If he could "do it over again," Norman would start lifting weights earlier in his career. He felt his most important workouts were early season 660s timed, and mid-season, a 400-300-200-100 over hurdles ladder.

Norman takes 24 steps to the first hurdle and 17 steps between hurdles, preferring to come out of the curve well placed in the race, then out-run the competition down the straightaway.

DAILY SEASONAL WORKOUTS
Fall

Monday—Stride 880 at ¾-speed for time.
Tuesday—Rest.
Wednesday—Jog 3 miles.
Thursday—Stride 880 at ¾-speed for time.
Friday—Rest.
Saturday—Rest.
Sunday—2-mile run at ½-speed for time.

Winter

Monday—3x660 under 1:45; hurdle work.
Tuesday—Run 880 between weight-lifting sets.
Wednesday—5-man continuous relays, each running 220 until everyone has run 10-12x220.
Thursday—Run 880 between weight-lifting sets.
Friday—Run 100s along sides of football field, walk across ends for recovery for 12 laps.
Saturday—Rest.
Sunday—Stride 880 at ¾-speed.

Spring

Monday—400-300-200-100 over hurdles ladder.
Tuesday—Run 880 between weight-lifting sets.
Wednesday—Hurdle ladder.
Thursday—Run 100s along sides of football field, walk across ends for recovery for 12 laps.
Friday—Stride 10xfootball field.
Saturday—Competition.
Sunday—Rest.

Summer

Monday—400 over hurdles; 4x150 over hurdles.
Tuesday—15-stride runs on grass; hurdlework.
Wednesday—6-8x150 over hurdles.
Thursday—10 stride runs on grass; hurdle work.
Friday—300 over hurdles—200-100 over hurdles—50 over hurdles.
Saturday—Stride 880 at ¾-speed.
Sunday—2 miles at ½-speed for time.

Coy West, Jr.

COY ELDRIDGE WEST JR.	Humble High School
Born 9/4/62	Humble, Texas
5-11 181	Coach Tom Jones

COMPETITIVE BACKGROUND

Coy first went out for track in junior high school in order to increase his speed for football. A top-ranking intermediate hurdler in Texas, he went on to set a national Junior Olympic record in the 400-meter hurdles.

BEST TIMES

9.9   22.0   48.8(m)   37.6(300LH)   52.92(400IH)
1:58.9(m)

AGE GROUP MARKS

Year	Age	100	300LH	400	400IH
1977	14		31.6(250LH)		
1978	15	11.0	41.2	54.2	
1979	16	10.4	38.7	50.3	
1980	17	9.9	37.5	48.8	52.92
1981	18	serious injury	38.8	50.4	

PREPARATION

Coy uses low weight-high repetition weight training for endurance and 4 sets of 5 reps at maximum weight for strength work.

Before practice and meets he jogs, stretches a great deal, and runs short sprints.

TRAINING COMMENTS

Coy feels that long distance work and good speed work have been very important, but for the hurdles, the perfection of minor details is the key. "Every aspect of training is important," he says. To perfect his skills, Coy uses a number of drills, his favorite having 3 hurdles placed one step apart; he then runs through with just his lead leg, then just his trail leg.

During football season of his senior year, Coy broke his leg and tore all of the ligaments in his ankle. Two operations repaired the leg with 7 screws and a 6"x1½" metal plate. Doctors told him it would be 6 months before he could run and a year before he could compete. Coy set his mind on a faster recovery; working hard with a bicycle, weights and stretching, he was able to compete 4 months later, running 52.0 for the 400 meters.

DAILY SEASONAL WORKOUTS
Fall and Winter
Monday—Long distance work; hurdle work.
Tuesday—Interval work.
Wednesday—200-300-400-550-400-300-200.
Thursday—6x200 over hurdles.
Friday—Jog 1-mile; sprint over hurdles; stretch.
Saturday—Distance work.
Sunday—Distance work.

Spring and Summer
Monday—Speedwork.
Tuesday—Distance run.
Wednesday—Hurdle work: start at the 300 mark and run over the 1st and 2nd hurdles.
Thursday—Hurdle work: start at the 200 mark and run over the 2nd and 3rd hurdle.
Friday—Jog; stretch; light hurdle work.
Saturday—Competition.
Sunday—Distance work.